Twelve Against The Gods
Lessons From The Classic Text

Roger Covington

Table of Contents

Preface

The core idea of this book is that greats throughout history are typically remembered for the one incredible thing at which they excelled often forgetting that many were absolute failures at most everything else. In this largely out-of-print classic, Bolitho hilariously depicts the rise and downfall of some of the most familiar names in world history. Through the book's obsession with failure and foible, he re-veals the human side of demigods, bringing them down to earth in a way that makes them more relatable. Bolitho picks several characters from the past and writes their lives in brief. The list is varied: Alexander the Great, Cagliostro, Christopher Columbus, Casanova, Charles XII of Sweden, Mohammed (spelled in the old style, as "Mahomet"), Lola Montez, Isadora Duncan, Catiline, Napoleon (I & III), and Woodrow Wilson. Bolitho is not hero-worshipping – the common thread uniting his portraits isn't selflessness or even physical bravery but rather an essential hunger for life, and a willingness to risk everything for that hunger.

Twelve Against the Gods is the kind of highly opinionated, actively moralizing after-dinner conversation starter that was the norm rather than the exception among the ancient writers Bolitho so adored. The theme of the book is the adventure of bucking established practices in pursuit of greatness. Bolitho noted that each of the book's subjects "fought against the conventions of their times, for better or for worse." You'll not likely find more entertaining books of historical essays in modern print. Bolitho's curiously baroque prose style is as original as his contagious irreverence for and astonishment at the lives of his subjects.

In this book, we present a summary of the key figures in Bolitho's classic and pull key lessons – both professional and personal – that we can learn from these towering figures. Although all the greats featured in the book lived ages ago, the principles by which they lived their lives hold valuable lessons for those of us in contemporary times. All were wildly successful in their chosen fields and we aim to distill key business, leadership and personal lessons from these. Each chapter delves into the life on one of the characters from the classic book, tracing their path to success (and ultimate ruin) while highlighting the key lessons to be gleaned. It is our fervent hope that you find value in these lessons and apply them to your per-sonal and professional success.

- Roger Covington

CHAPTER 1

ALEXANDER THE

GREAT

Alexander the Great was a King of the Ancient Greek kingdom of Macedon and a member of the Argead dynasty. He was born in Pella in 356 BC. During his youth, the philosopher Aristotle tutored Alexander until the age of 16. After King Philip's assassination in 336 BC, Alexander succeeded his father to the throne and inherited a strong kingdom and an experienced army. He spent most of his ruling years on an unprecedented military campaign through Asia and northeast Africa, and by the age of thirty, he had created one of the largest empires of the ancient world, stretching from Greece to northwestern India.

He was undefeated in battle and is widely considered one of history's most successful military commanders.

Alexander was awarded the generalship of Greece and used this authority to launch his father's PanHellenic project to lead the Greeks in the conquest of Persia. In 334 BC he invaded the Achaemenid Empire, ruled Asia Minor, and began a series of campaigns that lasted ten years. Alexander broke the power of Persia in a series of decisive battles, most notably the battles of Issus and Gaugamela. He subsequently overthrew the Persian King Darius III and conquered the Achaemenid Empire in its entirety. At that point, his empire stretched from the Adriatic Sea to the Indus River.

Seeking to reach the "ends of the world and the Great Outer Sea", he invaded India in 326 BC, but was eventually forced to turn back at the demand of his troops. Alexander died in Babylon in 323 BC, the city he planned to establish as his capital, without executing a series of planned campaigns that would have begun with an invasion of Arabia. In the years following his death, a series of civil wars tore his empire apart, resulting in several states ruled by the Diadochi, Alexander's surviving generals and heirs.

Alexander's legacy includes the cultural diffusion his conquests engendered, such as Greco-Buddhism. He founded some twenty cities that bore his name, most notably Alexandria in Egypt. Alexander's settlement of Greek colonists and the resulting spread of Greek culture in the east resulted in a new Hellenistic civilization, aspects of which were still evident in the traditions of the Byzantine Empire in the mid-15th century and the presence of Greek speakers in central and far eastern Anatolia until the 1920s. Alexander became the measure against which military leaders compared themselves, and military academies throughout the world still teach his tactics.

Alexander the Great was trained from birth to be a conqueror and he lived up to his destiny. He was appointed King at the age of 20 and in the twelve short years before his death would conquer most of the known world. Alexander was un-defeated in battle despite being at a numerical disadvantage in numerous battles and is debatably the greatest conqueror in world history. His father left him a strong kingdom ready for expansion and prepared him to lead it. He was trusted with crushing revolts and leading by proxy at a young age while his father waged war which helped prepare him for his future.

Key Lessons:

Seek Out the Best Mentors...Then Learn from Them

Alexander had the benefit of being educated in political, military, and cultural matters by excellent tutors including none other than Aristotle. He also accompanied his father on several military campaigns and distinguished himself in battle at a young age. He no doubt drew upon that upbringing when he assumed the throne at only 20 years old after Philip was assassinated. Alexander wasted no time in using his position as general of all Greece to take the strong army his father had left him and expand Greek hegemony into Persia. The lesson here is to prepare yourself by being open to what others more senior can teach you. They've been where you are, and they are where you want to be. Adopting an attitude of continual learning from those you respect will make you a better leader.

Seize the opportunity when your time comes

Alexander's mentor and father Philip was assassinated. Alexander had to act boldly and consolidate power to avoid letting his destiny slip through his grasp. His-tory is replete with stories of great generals—heroes who saved their men, their cities, and their countries. It is equally populated with those who failed in their task, sometimes spectacularly. These are often those who fail to seize the moment.

Be flexible in your decision-making

Alexander's conquests brought him into contact with a wide variety of armies and cultures. To deal with the ever-changing military, political, cultural, and economic landscape, he planned meticulously, analyzed every piece of information and formulated as many alternatives as possible. From a military standpoint, such efforts reduced his risk, increased his flexibility, and enabled him to operate with speed and decisiveness with his highly trained and exceptionally loyal army. The lesson here is that a flexible and adaptable strategy is a crucial element to success as a leader. Systematic planning, a comprehensive view, and incorporating a range of options allows you to change your strategy depending on the situation and environment you face. In so doing, you can put together a strategy that will serve you well.

A Winning Strategy is Both Efficient and Innovative

Amazingly, Alexander built his empire with an army that numbered no more than 40,000 men. This means he had to employ his forces to overcome the over-whelming numbers that opposed him. Toward that end, he used terrain, tactics, mobility, and weaponry—including the formidable Macedonian phalanx—to over-whelm his opponents. In addition, since he could ill afford to detach men from his army to secure his rear lines of communication, he was extraordinarily sympathetic to the people he conquered, going so far as to adopt their dress and customs and even build memorials to their war dead. The lesson here is that Like Alexander, you can focus on your core capabilities that you need to get the job done. Work to resource those capabilities as efficiently as you can while also being innovative in how you do it. For instance, use your negotiation skills to build mutually satisfying alliances that enhance your ability to carry out your strategy.

The Perils of Professional Excess and Personal Dissipation

As time went on, Alexander's ambition began to grow into megalomania, a megalomania fueled by heavy drinking. As his mood became progressively more violent and unstable, those around him came to fear the repercussions of his anger. As he advanced farther East, Alexander's mental stability progressively eroded. Despite the grave misgivings of his close advisors, he asserted himself as a god. He also held elaborate drinking parties called "symposiums" where wine flowed freely and court sycophants told him how great he was. Alexander drank to stupefying excesses. As a leader in a position of power, you are vulnerable to physical strains, psychological stress, and an oversized ego.

Alexander used alcohol and an obsessive pursuit of conquest to sustain himself, and likewise, many other unhealthy substitutes are available to you: like working long hours, fomenting intrigue, and walking over your people. But you have a choice to be a leader with integrity who does the right thing for yourself, your people, and your organization. This includes taking care of your physical and mental health. The role you play and the responsibilities you have demand no less.

Have A Compelling Vision, Be Good At Execution And Be True To Your Word

Alexander's actions demonstrate what can be accomplished when a person is totally focused—when he or she has clarity coupled with a 'magnificent obsession'. Through dramatic gestures and great rhetorical skills, Alexander spoke to the collective imagination of his people and won the commitment of his followers. Alexander not only had a compelling vision, he also knew how to make that vision be-come reality. By maintaining an excellent information system, he was able to interpret his opponent's motives and was a master at coordinating all parts of his military machine. No other military leader before him ever used speed and surprise with such dexterity. He knew the true value of the statement "One is either quick or one is dead!" Alexander set the example of excellence with his leadership style; he led his troops quite literally from the front. When his troops went hungry or thirsty, he went hungry and thirsty; when their horses died beneath them and they had to walk, he did the same. This accessibility only changed when he succumbed to the luxury of Persian court life.

Encourage Innovation, Foster Group Identification And Encourage And Support Your Followers

Alexander realized the competitive advantage of strategic innovation. Because of his deft deployment of troops, his support for and reliance on the creativity of his corps of engineers, and his own logistical acumen, his war machine was the most advanced of its time. Alexander created a very astute propaganda machine to keep his people engaged. His oratory skills, based on the simple language of his soldiers, had a hypnotic influence on all who heard him. He made extensive use of powerful cultural symbols which elicited strong emotions. These 'meaning-management' actions, combined with his talent for leading by example, fostered strong group identification among his troops, and motivated his men to make exceptional efforts. Alexander knew how to encourage his people for their excellence in battle in ways that brought out greater excellence. He routinely singled people out for special attention and recalled acts of bravery performed by former and fallen heroes, making it clear that individual contributions would be recognized. He also had the ability to be a 'container' of the emotions of his people through empathetic listening.

Invest In Talent Management, Consolidate Gains And Plan For The Future

Extremely visionary for his time, Alexander spent an extraordinary amount of resources on training and development. He not only trained his present troops but also looked to the

future by developing the next generation. Paradoxically, three of Alexander's most valuable lessons were taught not through his strengths but through his weaknesses. The first of these is the need to consolidate gains. Alexander failed to put the right control systems in place to integrate his empire and thus never really savored the fruit of his accomplishments. Conquest may be richly re-warding, but a leader who advances without ensuring the stability of his or her gains stands to lose everything. Another lesson Alexander taught by omission is the need for a viable succession plan. He was so focused on his own role as king and aspiring deity that he could not bring himself to think of the future when he was gone. As a result, political vultures tore his vast empire apart after his death.

CHAPTER 2

GIACOMO

CASANOVA

Giacomo Girolamo Casanova was an Italian adventurer and author from Venice. His autobiography, Histoire de ma vie (Story of My Life), is regarded as one of the most authentic sources of the customs and norms of European social life during the 18th century. He has become famous for his often complicated and elaborate affairs with women that his name is now synonymous with "womanizer". Poor, ambitious, and handsome, Casanova was one of those people who always seemed to be at the right place at the right time. He saved the Venetian senator Zuan Bragadino from a fall down a staircase in 1746 and thereafter enjoyed a measure of political protection for his shady activities, for which he was already acquiring a reputation. Under his tutelage, Casanova visited France, Germany, and Austria, hawking a peculiar blend of esoteric knowledge, medical cures, and occult magic. His language skills and innate charm enabled him to float among clerics, socialites, royalty, and wealthy businessmen. Sentenced to prison for five years in Venice for teaching occult wisdom and disturbing the peace, he escaped after fifteen months (1757). He was able to attach himself to wealthy women by peddling the healing and magical arts, and added significantly to his income by cheating at cards and other games of chance.

Throughout his travels around Europe, he accumulated numerous mistresses and sired progeny here and there as opportunity would have it. His seductive self-assurance, alleged "occult" knowledge, and unusual ability to win at casino games, earned him access to the highest social circles in the countries he visited, but sooner or later he always found himself either in jail or escorted to the frontier. Like all great seducers, he was possessed of a powerful intellect, which he was able to deploy on his targets when needed. And he had the daring and flair that comes from a man who has nothing to lose. He claimed even to have met and de-bated philosophy and religion with Voltaire, the great intellect of the age. If we are to believe his account of the debate with Voltaire, Casanova even came out ahead in the exchange. He fought duels with angry rivals now and then, but ac-cording to him, of course, he always won.

After various adventures and assorted sexual conquests too numerous to re-count, he eventually discovered that his ruses, wit, and sleight-of-hand had reached the point of diminishing returns. He eventually accepted a position as a librarian at a castle in Bohemia, which was crushingly boring but at least stable and secure. There he spent the last fourteen years of his life in dreary book-lined drudgery, writing his memoirs ten to twelve hours per day as a way of relieving the solitude of his existence. He claims absolute honesty in his narrative, and much of it actually agrees with history.

Key Lessons:

A Detached, Ironic View Of Life Is The Best Refuge.

Casanova likes to pretend that the hardships he endured (poor background, lack of family and permanent love) did not touch his emotions. He suppresses his feelings, and takes refuge in witty comments and philosophical statements. Not sure whether to believe in God or not? Then just employ Pascal's Wager, and all will be well, Casanova suggests. (Pascal's Wager, named after the French philosopher Blaise Pascal, is a name given to a sort of "cost-benefit" argument used to justify belief in God. Very basically, it says that since we will never know whether God exists or not, it makes more sense to believe in the existence of a deity, since the benefits of belief outweigh the disadvantages of belief).

Strive For An Extraordinary Life.

Casanova never apologizes for any of his frauds, schemes, and trickery he did in his life. He definitely gives the impression that, although he regrets how he ended up, his personality would not have let things turn out any other way. Normal life was a soul-destroying charade anyway, he apparently believed, so a little fraud now and then would never hurt anyone.

Character Determines Fate.

This idea goes back as far as the Greek tragedians. Casanova knows that he could not escape his true nature, no matter how hard he tried. He appears to have discovered things about himself he would rather not have known at certain times in his life, and this knowledge sent him further down the path where he ended up. Basically, he had a stoic fatalism that suggested the wheels of fate grind on regardless of a man's plans or needs. He ended up as he did because his character made it inevitable.

Always Remember To Have Fun.

Regardless how he ended up, Casanova packed several lifetimes of adventure into his years on this earth. He knows this very well, and always slyly suggests that it was all worth it. While he never advocated unrestrained debauchery, there is little doubt that he structured his life around the pursuit of sensual delights.

Alienation Is Inescapable.

Casanova takes delight in relating how he outwitted the wealthy aristocrats he came into contact with. He, from a poor background, could not help but notice how alienated and separated he was from the people he mixed with. No matter how hard he tried to integrate himself into proper society, it never worked. Casa-nova was the consummate outsider, condemned to live his existence on the mar-gins. He was arguably the first red-pill ingester. And he knew it.

CHAPTER 3

CHRISTOPHER COLUMBUS

Christopher Columbus was an Italian explorer, navigator, colonizer, and citizen of Genoa. Under the auspices of the Catholic Monarchs of Spain, he completed four voyages across the Atlantic Ocean. Those voyages, and his efforts to establish permanent settlements on the island of Hispaniola, initiated the European colonization of the New World. In the context of emerging western imperialism and economic competition among European kingdoms through the establishment of trade routes and colonies, Columbus's proposal to reach the East Indies by sailing westward eventually received the support of the Spanish Crown, which saw in it a chance to enter the spice trade with Asia through a new westward route. During his first voyage in 1492, instead of arriving at Japan as he had intended, he reached the New World, landing on an island in the Bahamas Archipelago that he named "San Salvador". Over the course of three more voyages, he visited the Greater and Lesser Antilles, as well as the Caribbean coast of Venezuela and Central America, claiming all of it for the crown of Castile.

Though Columbus was not the first European explorer to reach the Americas (having been preceded by the Vikinger expedition led by Leif Erikson in the 11th century) his voyages led to the first lasting European contact with the Americas, inaugurating a period of European exploration, conquest, and colonization that lasted for several centuries. These voyages had, therefore, an enormous impact on the historical development of the modern Western world. He spearheaded the transatlantic slave trade and has been accused by several historians of initiating the genocide of the Hispaniola natives. Columbus himself saw his accomplishments primarily in the light of spreading the Christian religion.

Key Lessons:

It Pays To Be Curious At Times.

This is true especially to the great Christopher Columbus, the man who discovered the American continent. He was truly an adventurous soul. If it wasn't for him, things would have been totally different today. He had a great mind for think-ing that the world is spherical in shape, opposite to what many others thought that it is flat.

There Are Always Opportunities, Even If Others Don't See Them.

Life has so much to offer, but your success depends on how you see life. For Christopher Columbus, he chooses to see every opportunity where others did not. The Europeans have traveled to China and India through a safe route. However, time came when the Ottoman Turks had invaded and ruled over the land, placing difficulties for travel. In this case, a new way to reach the place has to be discovered. Before, the populace believed that there was only one way to reach China and India, but Christopher Columbus was wise enough to use the westerly route, rather than passing through the tip of South Africa. The westerly route was in-deed shorter and easier to use for travel. Unlike the popular stereotype, there was an accepted belief that the world was, in fact, round and not flat during Columbus's day. However, no one had accurately measured its circumference or correctly gauged distances between landmasses: that is, until Columbus. Someone has to challenge the norm, disprove untruths, and propose new ideas, if growth and change are to occur. This life lesson is also similar to the common note of thinking outside the box. Many people may think alike, making one idea to be a social norm since the majority believes in it. On the contrary, that single idea may not be absolutely right. Sometimes, people choose a path because one person said it's the right one. However, there actually is a better road that no one is too confident to pass. This boils down to our choices. It is, therefore, important to lay out all possibilities and chose the one that yields the most benefits. Some others may not see your idea as the best, but you should try following your own, for you are sure of tasting your success at the end of the road.

Always Trust Yourself

Columbus once said that "You can never cross the ocean unless you have the courage to lose sight of the shore." That first step forward is always the most difficult. Human as we are, we are never perfect. However, life has given us the endless abilities and the power to think. Using our minds, we should be able to strengthen our faith and make sure that we make the right decisions, not because others tell us to, but because that's the way we want it to happen. Human intuition does not exist for nothing. When Christopher Columbus was on his way to Asia through the westerly route, he knew that he was on the right track and that land was not far from where they are located since he saw birds in the sky and some vegetation floating on the waters. Christopher Columbus' journeys teach us to set goals and keep our eyes on that goal. We have to keep a good vision and aim to reach for them always. Most of the successful individuals from any generation have succeeded because they never lost their hope.

They have held tighter onto their dreams. Even though the dreams were simple, they never let go of it. Instead, they have worked on them and believed that they will be able to reach it, and so they did. There were challenges along the way, but Columbus stayed the course, even after the success of his first journey. He set sail again and again, determined to continue his mission of exploration and learning. It is what we must do to be successful in art, in leadership, in our callings, and in life.

Confidence Pays.

Once you trust yourself fully, it would then be easier for you to be confident in the things that you normally do. It is important for an individual to be able to trust himself in whatever he does. This will help you reach your goal and actually help in attracting more money for business. If you are planning to put up or are already managing a business, you should be confident enough to look after the tasks that need to be done. When you are self-assured, it will be easier to attract investors and customers to your business. We tend to want to do things on our own and ask for help only if we are in a jam. But not Columbus. He recognized that he would need support for his explorations and boldly asked for help again and again. In fact, the title Columbus proposed for himself was "Great Admiral of the Ocean." In hindsight, that may seem a bit arrogant. Not so. Great risk should bring great reward. Had Columbus not had the confidence in his mission, he would not have been successful, either at circumnavigating the globe or in finally convincing Ferdinand and Isabella to finance the trip after many other failed attempts with other leaders.

There Will Always Be Doubting People.

When Christopher Columbus formed his theory that sailing west would reach their trade destinations faster, he was met with great doubt. Many people still believed the world was flat, and that sailing too far west would result in Columbus simply falling off the face of the earth, literally. Those who knew the world was round thought the earth was far too big to make it by sailing west. They would be out at sea way too long and would die before reaching India or China. As entrepreneurs, you will also be faced with many doubts about your ideas and business. We live in a culture that thinks starting a business is risky. People don't like you trying things they can't do themselves. As a result, your efforts will often be met with doubt and resistance, even from well-meaning friends and family. Great businesses, like discoveries, are made in the midst of doubt.

Failure Is Valuable

Christopher Columbus thought that by sailing west, he would discover a better trade route to China and India. Fortunately, this idea failed and Columbus did not reach India and China. Instead, he discovered an entire new world. You too will likely fail in your first ideas for your business. Chances are, your success will look nothing like you originally envision it. And that's OK. Successful entrepreneurs learn to pivot when their initial plans fall through and often find success in areas they never even imaged when they started. Your first idea will probably fail, but if you learn to adapt, you will find success you never imagined in the beginning.

Everyone Has Something To Teach

Christopher Columbus and his men did some bad things to the people living in the lands they discovered. As the stories of their cruelty become public knowledge, there has been a push by some groups to no longer celebrate Christopher Columbus and his discoveries. This is nonsense. Just because someone did bad things at some point doesn't mean we shouldn't celebrate and try to learn from the great things they did. History is full of men and women who achieved amazing things. Many of these same people also did some really bad things. If we are going to throw out all the successful people who did bad things at some point in their lives, we are missing golden learning opportunities. I'm currently reading Al Capone's biography and learning a ton of business ideas from him, despite the fact that he was one of the most evil gangsters of all time. When it comes to mentors, whether in person or just ones you read about in books, learn to take the good and throw out the bad in their successes.

CHAPTER 4

PROPHET

MOHAMMED

Mohammad (or Muhammad) the central figure of Islam and widely regarded as its founder by non-Muslims. Muslims know him as the "Holy Prophet", almost all of whom. Consider him to be the last prophet sent by God to mankind to restore Is-lam, which they believe to be the unaltered original monotheistic faith of Adam, Abraham, Moses, Jesus, and other prophets.He united Arabia into a single Muslim polity and ensured that his teachings, practices, and the Quran, which Muslims believe was revealed to him by God, formed the basis of Islamic religious belief. Born in the Arabian city of Mecca, in approximately 570 CE, Muhammad was orphaned at an early age; he was raised under the care of his paternal uncle Abu Talib. Periodically he would retreat to a cave named Hira in the mountains for several nights of seclusion and prayer; later, at age 40, he reported being visited by Gabriel in the cave, where he stated he received his first revelation from God.

Three years after this event Muhammad started preaching these revelations publicly, proclaiming that "God is One", that complete "surrender" to him is the only way acceptable to God, and that he was a prophet and messenger of God, similar to the other prophets in Islam. Muhammad gained few early followers, and met hostility from some Meccan tribes. To escape persecution, Muhammad sent some followers to Abyssinia before he and his followers migrated from Mecca to Medina (then known as Yathrib) in the year 622. This event, the Hijra, marks the beginning of the Islamic calendar, also known as the Hijri Calendar. In Medina, Muhammad united the tribes under the constitution of Medina. In December 629, after eight years of intermittent conflict with Meccan tribes, Muhammad gathered an army of 10,000 Muslim converts and marched on the city of Mecca. The attack went largely uncontested and Muhammad seized the city with little bloodshed. He destroyed 360 pagan idols at the Kaaba. In 632, a few months after returning from the Farewell Pilgrimage, Muhammad fell ill and died. Before his death, most of the Arabian Peninsula had converted to Islam.

Key Lessons:

Be Honest In Your Affairs

The Holy Prophet (P.B.U.H) was extremely honest and trustworthy in his day-to-day affairs. This was a rare quality in the era he lived, when merchants and vendors used to swindle and deceive the consumers for petty profits. When he left on a trade journey, his female employer at the time Hazrat Khadija (R.A) sent an-other employee to accompany the Holy Prophet (P.B.U.H) to observe the way he dealt her goods. His findings indicated that Khadija's (R.A) business was being handled by the Prophet (P.B.U.H) with utmost diligence and sincerity.

Upon return, the Prophet Muhammad (P.B.U.H) came bearing handsome prof-its on account of his honest dealings. This unique characteristic of Holy Prophet (P.B.U.H) impressed her so much that later on she sent him a proposal of marriage which ultimately Prophet Muhammad (P.B.U.H) accepted.

Uphold The Truth

Before that miraculous night when the Holy Prophet (P.B .U.H) was appointed as the final Messenger, the whole city of Makkah called him by the worthy names of Al-Sadiq, Al-Amin (The Honest, The Trustworthy). This not only placed the people's firm belief and trust in him but when he finally began to preach the religion of God, people adhered to his attestations.

Be Dedicated

The Holy Prophet (P.B.U.H) was so focused on his mission to propagate the word of God that he was ready to bear every hardship that came his way. When the affluent in Makkah came to realize that he was becoming popular among the masses, they chose to offer him incentives so that he gave up preaching the message of Islam. He was offered worldly possessions such as wealth, status of the chief of Makkah and marriage to the most beautiful woman at the time. Yet he remained steadfast towards his purpose and remarked, "Even if they place the sun in my right hand and the moon in my left, I will not renounce my mission until I die or God fulfills my mission for me."

Be Compassionate

The Prophet's message was not well received by all. Those who were too en-grossed in idol worship refused to listen to his voice of reason and logic, started causing him physical pain and injury. His own uncle Abu Lahab's wife scattered thorns in his path yet he never responded back but simply changed his course. A woman used to throw trash on him every day when he walked past her house but the noble Prophet (P.B.U.H) never rebuked her instead when one day the woman did not show up to throw trash at him, it prompted him to visit her house. Finding her ill and bed ridden, he was kind to her and inquired after her health. The woman was thoroughly ashamed of her actions and repented at once, accepting Islam. This is how the prophet used his merciful trait to conquer his enemies and convert them into his well wishers.

Lead By Example

He was always a role model and example for his followers. In the famous battle of the Trench, the Muslims were outnumbered and awfully short on supplies. Hunger and suffering were common during those times. A companion once came to the Prophet (P.B.U.H) and complained regarding his hunger and pointed to a stone fastened around his stomach to prevent hunger. The Holy Prophet (P.B.U.H) lifted his shirt and pointed towards not one but two stones fastened to his own stomach.

CHAPTER 5

LOLA MONTEZ

Marie Dolores Eliza Rosanna Gilbert, Countess of Landsfeld (17 February 1821 – 17 January 1861), better known by the stage name Lola Montez, was an Irish dancer and actress who became famous as a "Spanish dancer", courtesan, and mis-tress of King Ludwig I of Bavaria, who made her Countess of Landsfeld. She used her influence to institute liberal reforms. At the start of the Revolutions of 1848 in the German states, she was forced to flee. She proceeded to the United States via Switzerland, France and London, returning to her work as an entertainer and lecturer.

There are contradictions and unknown facts surrounding the fascinating life of Lola Montez. Lola herself through two small autobiographies generated many of these. She also wrote several performance scripts about her own life. She claimed to have been born in Limerick Ireland on June 23, 1818. At least that is the date on her tombstone, but her birth certificate came to light in the late 1990s correct-ing the first of many misconceptions about Lola. Eliza Rosanna Gilbert was born to Elizabeth Oliver and Edward Gilbert February 17, 1821. Elizabeth was four-teen when she married Edward on April 29, 1820 in Cork, Ireland, so it's clear that Elizabeth was not pregnant with Eliza when she married as some have alleged. Edward, an Ensign in the 25th Foot Regiment was stationed in India in 1823 and took his family with him. Later that year, he died of cholera, and Elizabeth soon married Lieutenant Patrick Craigie.

Both her father and stepfather were good to Eliza, but when she was sent to Scotland for school, she didn't adjust very well. She first lived with Craigie's father, then with his sister, and then was sent to boarding school. One of her teachers de-scribed her as elegant, graceful, and beautiful, with an "air of haughty ease." She was also extravagant, impetuous, and had a violent temper. But at this point, her misbehavior was limited to putting flowers in the wig of the man in front of her in church, and supposedly running through the streets naked.

When Eliza was reunited with her mother in 1837, her mother proposed an arranged marriage with a 64 year old widower. Her response was to elope with 31 year old Lieutenant Thomas James. Eliza and Thomas were properly married in Dublin by his brother, and headed back to India where Thomas was stationed. The marriage didn't last long, however. We don't know which of them, if either, strayed from the marriage, but when Lola left India, she took up with George Lennox on the ship on the way home. They were not very discreet and were observed both on the ship and in a London hotel together.

At the age of 20, Eliza, or Mrs. Betty James as she called herself, was estranged from her mother and had begun to develop a scandalous reputation by eloping, abandoning her husband, and then having an illicit affair. She also needed a way to support herself, so she decided to become a Spanish dancer. She took dance lessons and then traveled to Spain to learn Spanish and Spanish dance. On June 3, 1843, she made her debut at Her Majesty's Theatre in London, billed as Donna Lola Montez.

Lola's talent was questionable, but she was considered to be extraordinarily beautiful with a fabulous figure. Unfortunately, someone in the audience who shouted her name calling her Betty James recognized her. Deciding that because of her reputation, London wasn't the right place to perform, she left and began to tour Europe. In 1844, she met and had an indiscreet affair with Franz Liszt, the Hungarian composer. When the affair died out, she decided to go to Paris.

In Paris, Lola's career was not successful, but she had some success as a courtesan beginning an affair with Alexander Dujarier, a young newspaper editor and owner. With Dujarier she was part of a literary crowd where she met and was ru-mored to have an affair with Alexander Dumas, pere. In 1845, Dujarier died in a duel unrelated to Lola. After the trial where his assailant was acquitted, she left Paris to go to Munich.

Presenting herself to the Bavarian court as a Spanish noblewoman, Lola became acquainted with King Ludwig I. He was captivated by her and made her his official mistress. Ludwig lavished gifts on Lola including a house with all the trappings and a substantial income. On his birthday, February 17, 1847, he went so far as to make her Countess Marie von Landsfeld, and bestow Bavarian citizenship on her.

Not content to be only a mistress, Lola began to give him advice about politics, typically siding with the middle class and students. This didn't sit well with his aristocratic advisers and councilors, but in time, Lola's extravagant lifestyle even turned the lower classes against her. Faced with evidence of her duplicity, Ludwig stood by her, but revolution was in the making and Lola was forced to flee the country after a mob destroyed much of her home. Eventually, Ludwig was forced to abdicate and go into exile. Although Lola continued to write passionate letters to Ludwig (and ask for money), they weren't reunited and Lola returned to Lon-don.

At this point, Lola's exploits were being followed in the press, and satirized in the theater. In April 1848 "Pas de Fascination, or Catching a Governor" premiered in London as "Lola Montez or Countess for an Hour" by J Sterling Coyne. When she returned to London, Lola may have kept a low profile, but that didn't stop her from marrying George Trafford Heald in 1848. The problem was, that al-though Thomas James had gotten an official separation from the Church of England, divorces at the time could only be granted by an act of Parliament, so Lola wasn't officially divorced. George's aunt became suspicious and brought a bigamy suit against her. With a warrant out for Lola's arrest the couple was forced to flee. For a couple of years, they lived in France and Spain, but soon the relationship faltered and Lola once again took off to reinvent herself, this time to the United States.

By this time, Lola was no longer an unknown. Her life had been widely re-ported in the English-speaking world. Nevertheless, she traveled and performed in the eastern US from 1851 to 1853 before heading off to San Francisco, arriving in May 1853. In July, Lola entered into her third "marriage" to a reporter named Pat-rick Purdy Hull. The marriage lasted less than 3 months and she bought a mine in northern California where she settled down for a while until 1855.

Lola had always been volatile, but her raving seemed to increase during this time. She was suffering from severe headaches and poor health. She specifically railed against the Jesuits, accusing them of trying to poison her and shooting at her. A number of humorous plays had been written about her life and performed in Europe, and these were performed in California. She also wrote her autobiography, which was filled with misinformation, possibly to try to counteract some of the negative things that had been written about her in the press and for the stage. It's possible that her delusions of grandeur and feelings of paranoia at this time were the result of syphilis spreading to her brain.

In June of 1855, Lola decided to resume her career with a tour of Australia. She met with mixed reviews. In Melbourne, the theater audience began to decline after a review saying that her performance was "utterly subversive to all ideas of public morality." At Castle Maine, however, she received rave encores from a crowd of miners and the members of the Municipal Council. At one point, she at-tacked a reporter with a bullwhip in response to a bad review. On May 22, 1856, Lola left Australia to return to San Francisco. On the return voyage, the man she had been involved with during her tour, and who had been acting as her manager, Frank Folland, fell overboard. It is unknown whether or not it was an accident or suicide, but his death seemed to have a profound impact on Lola. She sold her jewelry and gave the money to Folland's children in an act that seemed out of character for her.

Either because of Folland's death, or because she was tired of the constant battles for the affection of the public, she gave up performing and began writing and lecturing, usually on topics related to beauty and the evils of Catholicism. She lectured in the US, Ireland, and London. Briefly, she tried to re-establish herself in London, but went into debt and fled creditors by returning to New York. For the last two years of her life, she joined the church and began the life of a reformer, working with prostitutes. She lived these years largely in poverty and after a series of strokes died on January 17, 1861. Her tombstone read Mrs. Eliza Gilbert.

Key Lessons:

Never Stop Learning

Learn from everyone and everything. Be like a kid in the candy store and learn from everybody around you. Everybody you know has their unique gifts. Learn from them, even if it means learning how NOT to do something. Also, people like to share what they're good at, so eat it up. Never be above learning, and learn from every one you can. Don't let your ego get in the way, no matter how smart you are. Focus on building your portable equity. Your day is filled with learning opportunities if you are open to them. You can teach an old dog new tricks. If you stay open. If you keep trying new things. You're growing or dying. There's no in-between. Never close your mind. Stay open to new worlds and new possibilities.

Invest In Yourself

This one will pay you back every time. You are your best investment, and you take you with you wherever you go. As Lola Montez says, "Investing in yourself is the best investment you will ever make. It will not only improve your life; it will improve the lives of all those around you." It's too easy when you finish school and start a job to say, "I'm done with learning." If you want to keep earning, you have to keep learning.

Drive From Your "WHY"

Every day you make a choice about how you show up in this world – at work, in your business, in life. Have a cause that drives you and a belief that inspires you. We fall short when we focus on what we do, and not what we stand for. Life's short. Then you die. Make it matter. Your purpose is power and it's fuel for your passion,

Drive From Your Purpose.

But where do you find it? Look inside. Find the answer to the question, "Why do you do what you do?" Peel away at an onion until you get to the inner core. Find your fire inside. That's where your strength to move mountains comes from, and your purpose is the torch that lights the way for others to help you in your cause.

Decide Who You Are

Define yourself. Don't let others define you or what you're capable of. My favorite answer to "Who are you?" is from Lola Montez: "You are what you learn."

Decide Who You Want To Be

Own your choice and live it like you mean it. One day when I was running around the halls at work, putting out fires, one of my mentors stopped me and asked, "How do you want others to experience you?" Not like a chicken with its head cut off. More like James Bond and on top of the situation. How do you want others to experience you? How do YOU want to experience you? Start from there, and drive from that. You'll immediately start creating more of the experiences that you want, and less of those that you don't.

Live YOUR Life

Who's life do you want to live? The one your parents or your friends want for you? Or, the one that fairy tales taught you? Or the life that the media tells you? It's your life. Live it on your terms. Don't live other people's lives. Don't try to keep up with the Joneses. Do what makes you happy. Know what you want, and what you need. Don't let other people's expectations for you rule your life, or limit the life that you want to lead. People pleasing wears you out, unless you find a way to please yourself first.

Live Your Life from the Inside Out

Start from the inside. Your outer world is a reflection of your inner world. We get what we project, and the world reflects back at us. Here are a few words of wisdom from Lola Montez:

"It's so easy to forget ultimates in the rush and hurry of daily life, especially for young people. So often, we're merely responders, so to speak, simply reacting to stimuli, to rewards and punishments, to emergencies, to pains and fears, to demands of other people, to superficialities. It takes a specific, conscious effort, at least at first, to turn one's attention to intrinsic things and values. Perhaps seeking actual physical aloneness. Perhaps exposing one's self to great music, to good people, to natural beauty, and so forth. Only after practice do these strategies become easy and automatic so that one can be living totally immersed in his or her river."

CHAPTER 6

ALESSANDRO

CAGLIOSTRO

Count Alessandro di Cagliostro was the alias of the occultist Giuseppe Balsa-mo (in French usually referred to as Joseph Balsamo). Cagliostro was an Italian ad-venturer and self-styled magician. He became a glamorous figure associated with the royal courts of Europe where he pursued various occult arts, including psychic healing and alchemy. His reputation lingered for many decades after his death, but continued to deteriorate, as he came to be regarded as a charlatan and impostor, this view fortified by the savage attack of Thomas

Carlyle (1795-1881) in 1833, who pronounced him the "Prince of Quacks". Later works—such as that of W.R.H. Trowbridge (1866-1938) in his Cagliostro: the Splendor and Misery of a Master of Magic (1910)—attempted a rehabilitation.

Giuseppe came from a poor family; his father was the son of a bookseller. Given the nature of history, there would be little cause to remember Balsamo had he not taken the assumed identity of Count Alessandro Cagliostro and embarked on a career of fakery, forgery, finagling and pharmacy. At least, that is what most historians believe. There are still some who find the proof for the bookseller's grandson to be somewhat tenuous and Cagliostro's deeds to be maligned. There is, indeed, evidence to suggest that the Count turned his hand to helping the destitute.

It would provoke little debate by suggesting that the young Balsamo was a talented youth. His poor, but educationally rich upbringing saw him educated in the Convento di San Rocco and in the Convento dei Fatebenefratelli di Caltagirone, although he tried to flee from both institutions and perpetually showed himself un-suited to formal education. Cagliostro's autobiography paints a different picture, with the Count unsurprisingly claiming noble birth, followed by being mysteriously abandoned on the island of Malta. His supposed childhood peregrinations took in Medina, Mecca and Cairo, with a return to Malta as a member of the Knights Hospitaller.

Balsamo, on the other hand, got into an altercation with a goldsmith called Marano over "hidden treasure" buried on the slopes of Monte Pellegrino. Let in on the expedition, thanks to a knowledge of herbs and magical rites, Giuseppe asked the smith for money. Needless to say, it seems the young swindler escaped to Messina with the actual rather than buried loot.

For those who want to follow the Cagliostro trail, there is a house in Palermo that purports to be the dwelling once inhabited by his family. In the now appropri-ately named, Vicolo Conte Cagliostro, in the heart of the Ballarò, is a house thought to be the birthplace of Giuseppe Balsamo. For the later periods in his life, at the height of his fame, you would have to look further afield including England and France.

The Count claimed that his first mentor of substance was a tutor called Altotas who initiated him into the ways of Eastern philosophy and alchemy. In Rome, his, or rather Balsamo's knowledge of the esoteric was put to nefarious use in the falsification of amulets and other more lucrative official documents. It seems that Gi-useppe's marriage to an ex-pat Sicilian and his conniving with the self-styled, marchese Alliata, led to nothing but trouble. The uncomfortable ménage moved to Bergamo and on to Aix-en-Provence where none other than Giacomo Casanova called him 'a lay-about genius who prefers a vagabond life to a hardworking existence' – the old phrase involving pots and kettles springs to mind at this point! Bal-samo also mixed in Rosicrucian circles, the secret society who followed the tenets set down by Christian Rosenkreuz in the middle Ages.

From France, the couple moved to Barcelona and Madrid, where beguiled by the fulsome attributes of Balsamo's wife, the marqués de Fontanar maintained them at his expense. All the while, at each stop on his extraordinary journey, Giuseppe was making contacts, creating a network of well-connected people. In 1772 the pair turned up in France, this time under the protection of a lawyer named Duplessis. Tired of being Balsamo's unofficial lure, his wife Lorenza Seraf-ina was attracted to the advocate for more than his status. Amidst claim and counter-claim, the unfortunate woman ended back by Cagliostro's side.

Whilst in France, Count Alessandro became well-known for his curative powers and his talismans. Bruno La Brasca, a Paris-based Cagliostro aficionado, to whom we're grateful for much information detailed here, quoted this piece concerning his ministrations towards the poor: '… Il prolonge la vie, secourt l'indigence. Le plaisir d'etre utile est sa seule récompense' (…He prolongs life, rescues the destitute. The pleasure of being useful is his only recompense). Maybe we should see Balsamo as a "Robin Hood" figure, hoodwinking the gullible rich with too much time on their hands.

It is in London that Cagliostro became definitively associated with the masons. He joined a lodge in a tavern in central London, specifically the Esperance in Gerrard Street. The Count is reputed to have created a masonic rite known as the Maçonnerie Egyptienne, which drew on ancient Egyptian ritual and references. Such esoteric learning put him firmly in the path of the Inquisition; unsurprisingly he finished up in Rome's Castel Sant' Angelo. He escaped a death sentence, but ended his days in the San Leo prison.

On his way to this ignominious conclusion to his eventful life, he was implicated in the "Affair of the diamond necklace", a complicated plot to defraud the French crown jewelers. It was a scandal that had wide-ranging political implications for a declining monarchy, in what was a time of austerity. Some big names were deeply tarnished by the affair, including Marie Antoinette, Cardinal Rohan and Jeanne de la Motte.

Rohan had been persuaded to purchase a very expensive necklace for the Queen, a necklace that Louis XV had originally commissioned for Madame du Barry. The Cardinal, in love with Marie Antoinette, believed he was meeting the Queen at Versailles; in fact, it was a hired prostitute dressed to resemble her. Encouraged by the meeting, he took the necklace, then on loan, to Marie Antoinette's go-between, who was really acting on behalf of de la Motte. She quickly spirited the diamonds away to England for her own gain.

The Countess de la Motte, perhaps to assuage her guilt, accused Cagliostro of being the brains behind the swindle. It was an allegation that saw him jailed in the Bastille. He escaped further punishment, owing to lack of evidence, but was banished from Paris. More details on the scandal can be found in Evelyne Lever's book, L'affaire du collier. Count Alessandro, however, sought exile in England, where he gave lessons in the alchemical arts. It was during this period that he was roundly denounced as Giuseppe Balsamo by the journalist, Théveneau de Morande, the type of scribbler who would have been very at home in the United Kingdom's current tabloid press. It was an accusation that Cagliostro always denied, but little concrete proof was ever offered to disprove it. Nevertheless, owing to the Count's published Open Letter to the English People, he received a retraction.

The curious life of Balsamo, aka Cagliostro, didn't end when he died. The vagaries and hidden depths of such a character were bound to be fodder for the literary and artistic imagination. He pops up as Sarastro in Mozart's Magic Flute; com-posers such as Johann Strauss and Claude Terrasse dedicated operas to him; the

German authors, Goethe and Schiller based works on his personality. Goethe even went in search of Balsamo's origins, a story he recounts in his Italian Journey. None other than Alexandre Dumas (père) had Joseph Balsamo as a character in several novels. He is almost as prevalent on the big screen, with Christopher Walken playing him in the 2001 film, The Affair of the Necklace.

One of the most interesting depictions comes from another author who buried his identity in a pseudonym, Luigi Natoli, also known as William Galt. Luigi was essentially an author of romanzi d'appendice, someone whose works often appeared in serial form in newspapers or magazines. He wrote more than 25 works in this manner, all set in Sicily. He is most well-known for a novel on the secretive secret, I Beati Paoli (The Blessed Paulists). Cagliostro was one of his other themes and translating the cover introduction can sum up his fictionalized account of the Count's life: 'Historical novel, memoir, tale of travel and adventure. The story of a man who lived his own life around the myth he had created for himself'. There is no better outline of Giuseppe Balsamo's life.

Unless someone uncovers a long-lost manuscript, it is extremely unlikely that the real story behind the smoke-screen of Cagliostro's career will ever be truly known. Perhaps it is the mystery that still draws us to this contradictory man, some-one capable of hoodwinking the rich, selling "snake oil" to the gullible, whilst continuing to indulge a more altruistic side.

Key Lessons:

Live Your Values

"Rather than love, than money, than fame, give me truth." — Henry David Thoreau

The key to The Good Life is spending more time in your values. To live your values, you need to know your values. When you know your values, you simply need to connect what you do each day back to your values. The smart way is to connect what you do at work to your values. For example, if you like to learn, then use each day as a learning opportunity, or a chance to master your craft. Or, if you value excellence, then raise the bar. Or, if you value beauty, then do more beautiful things and produce more works of art.

Drive from Your Life Style

For so many people, life makes more sense when they find a job where they can spend more time in their values and matches what they want their life style to be. If you don't like to travel, then don't choose a job that requires a lot of travel. If you don't want to work crazy hours, then don't choose a job where a crazy schedule comes with the territory and is the nature of the beast. It's easy to fall into the trap of chasing the idea that the grass is greener, or that the glory of the job is worth it, or that climbing the ladder will make life so much better. Then reality hits. Going up the ladder, doesn't necessarily mean spending more time doing what you love. Going up the ladder, doesn't mean life gets better or easier. In fact, it often means more sacrifice and more responsibility that you might not want at this point in your life. Worse, it might mean you spend a lot less time doing what you love and spending a lot less time in your strengths. Be careful what you wish for, because you just might get it.

Be Yourself

"Be who you are and say what you feel, because those who mind don't matter, and those who matter don't mind." - Bernard M. Baruch

Besides the fact that everybody else is taken, you're the best person for the job. But don't "just be yourself." Really, bring out yourself. Know what you bring to the table and how to flex what you've got. Share your unique gifts with the world, by spending more time in your strengths. Do more of YOUR art. Live your values. Know YOUR wants and needs. Stay true to you. The more authentic you are, the stronger you'll be in everything you do.

Know Thyself

"He who knows others is wise; he who knows himself is enlightened." — Lao Tzu

To be yourself, you need to know yourself, and what you're capable of. And, limitations, and opportunities for growth, too. The more you know yourself, the more you grow yourself, and the more you can bring out your best. And, the more you know yourself, the more you can also understand and appreciate others, and deal with differences. This will help you connect better and build better bridges.

Be Your Own Best Friend

"You're always with yourself, so you might as well enjoy the company." — Diane Von Furstenberg

If there's one person to have in your corner, it's you. Be your best coach, not your worst critic. You take you with you wherever you go, so it's worth figuring out how to lift yourself up, not beat yourself up, and how to have a strong sense of self-worth. The more compassionate you are with yourself, the more compassion-ate you'll be with others, and you get what you give. If you don't think your worth it, here's new for you …What separates the people that have a strong sense of love and belonging from those that don't? They think they're worth it. That's it. The choice is yours.

CHAPTER 7

CHARLES XII OF

SWEDEN

Charles XII belonged to the House of Palatinate-Zweibrücken, a branch line of the House of Wittelsbach. Charles was the only surviving son of Charles XI and Ulrika Eleonora the Elder. He assumed power, after a seven-month caretaker government, at the age of fifteen. In 1700, a triple alliance of Denmark–Norway, Saxony–Poland–Lithuania and Russia launched a threefold attack on the Swedish protectorate of Swedish Holstein-Gottorp and provinces of Livonia and Ingria, aiming to draw advantage as Sweden was unaligned and ruled by a young and inexperienced king, thus initiating the Great Northern War.

Leading the Swedish army against the alliance Charles won multiple victories despite being usually significantly outnumbered. A major victory over a Russian army some three times the size in 1700 at the Battle of Narva compelled Peter the Great to sue for peace which Charles then rejected. By 1706 Charles, now 24 years old, had forced all of his foes into submission including, in that year, a decisively devastating victory by Swedish forces under general Carl Gustav Rehnskiöld over a combined army of Saxony and Russia at the Battle of Fraustadt. Rus-sia was now the sole remaining hostile power.

Charles' subsequent march on Moscow met with initial success as victory followed victory, the most significant of which was the Battle of Holowczyn where the smaller Swedish army routed a Russian army twice the size. The campaign ended with disaster when the Swedish army suffered heavy losses to a Russian force more than twice its size at Poltava, a wound prior to the battle rendering him unable to take command had incapacitated Charles. The defeat was followed by Surrender at Perevolochna.

Charles spent the following years in exile in the Ottoman Empire before return-ing to lead an assault on Norway, trying to evict the Danish king from the war once more in order to aim all his forces at the Russians. Two campaigns met with frustration and ultimate failure, concluding with his death at the Siege of Fredriksten in 1718. At the time, most of the Swedish Empire was under foreign military occupation, though Sweden itself was still free. This situation was later formalized, albeit moderated in the subsequent Treaty of Nystad. The close would see not only the end of the Swedish Empire but also of its effectively organized absolute monarchy and war machine, commencing a parliamentarian government unique for continental Europe, which would last for half a century until royal autocracy was restored by Gustav III.

Charles was an exceptionally skilled military leader and tactician as well as an able politician, credited with introducing important tax and legal reforms. As for his famous reluctance towards peace efforts, Voltaire as saying upon the outbreak of the war quotes him; "I have resolved never to start an unjust war but never to end a legitimate one except by defeating my enemies". With the war consuming more than half his life and nearly all his reign, he never married and fathered no children, and was succeeded by his sister Ulrika Eleonora, who in turn was coerced to hand over all substantial powers to the Riksdag of the Estates and opted to surrender the throne to her husband, who became King Frederick I of Sweden.

Key Lessons:

Seek Simplicity

Simplify. It's way easy to make things more complex than they need to be. Seek simplicity. Simplicity is the key to sustainability. Drive towards it. If you keep things simple, you can better adapt to change. You can also focus more on what's important without getting lost in distractions and weeds.

Measure Your Life by the People Whose Lives You Touch

"Five hundred twenty - five thousand six hundred minutes ."

If you've seen Rent, you know the song and that's the number of minutes in a year. The song continues … "525,600 minutes – how do you measure, measure a year? … In daylights, in sunsets, in midnights, in cups of coffee. … In inches, in miles, in laughter, in strife. In 525,600 minutes – how do you measure a year in the life?"

How do you measure your life? You don't measure it in mansions or yachts. And, you don't need to climb a mountain to find the truth. You can measure your life by the people whose lives you touch.

Embrace the Challenge

You know the saying, "Easy come, easy go." And, "Whatever doesn't kill you makes you stronger." Do the tough stuff. Embrace the effort. It's how you grow. You'll often look back and you'll be proud of yourself for all those moments and all those times where you leaned in to your challenges, and gave it all you got. For so many things in life, you'll need to remind yourself the following: It's not easy. But, it's worth it.

Never Give Up

"If you're going through Hell, keep going." – Winston Churchill

Giving up is easy. Don't. Keep getting up to bat. Never shut down for good. It's not how hard you fall. It's how high you bounce. When you fall, get up again. As the saying goes, "Fall seven times, stand up eight."

Focus on What You Control, and Let the Rest Go

Every time life feels out of control, remind yourself to focus on what you control. And, let the rest go. When you act on what you control, you build momentum. More importantly, when you exercise the things within your control, you re-mind yourself that you are powerful and resourceful.

Take Action

"Life is like a game of chess. To win you have to make a move." — Allan Rufus, The Master's Sacred Knowledge

As Tony Robbins reminds us, "It's not knowing what to do, it's doing what you know."

Our power is our ability to act. Exercise it. Life's not static. Lead a life of action. Taking action helps you deal with change. A lot of success in life is about reducing the gap between knowing what to do, and actually doing what you know. Taking action keeps you from wallowing in misery, and it helps build momentum. If you're worried that you missed the boat, remind yourself of this timeless Chinese proverb: "The best time to plant a tree was 20 years ago. The second best time is now."

CHAPTER 8

NAPOLEON BONAPARTE

Napoléon Bonaparte was a French military and political leader who rose to prominence

during the French Revolution and led several successful campaigns during the Revolutionary Wars. As Napoleon I, he was Emperor of the French from 1804 until 1814, and again in 1815. Napoleon dominated European and global affairs for more than a decade while leading France against a series of coalitions in the Napoleonic Wars. He won most of these wars and the vast majority of his battles, building a large empire that ruled over continental Europe before its final collapse in 1815. One of the greatest commanders in history, his wars and campaigns are studied at military schools worldwide. He also remains one of the most celebrated and controversial political figures in human history.

Napoleon had an extensive and powerful influence on the modern world, bringing liberal reforms to the numerous territories that he conquered and controlled, especially the Low Countries, Switzerland, and large parts of modern Italy and Germany. He implemented fundamental liberal policies in France and throughout Western Europe. His lasting legal achievement, the Napoleonic Code, has influenced the legal systems of more than 70 nations around the world. British historian Andrew Roberts claimed, "The ideas that underpin our modern world— meritocracy, equality before the law, property rights, religious toleration, modern secular education, sound finances, and so on—were championed, consolidated, codified and geographically extended by Napoleon. To them he added a rational and efficient local administration, an end to rural banditry, the encouragement of science and the arts, the abolition of feudalism and the greatest codification of laws since the fall of the Roman Empire."

Napoleon was born in Corsica to a relatively modest family from the minor nobility. He supported the French Revolution from the outset while serving in the French army, and tried to spread its ideals to his native Corsica. He rose rapidly through the ranks during the Revolution, ending up as commander of the Army of Italy after saving the governing Directory by suppressing a revolt from royalist insurgents. At age 26, he began his first military campaign against the Austrians and their Italian allies, scoring a series of decisive victories, conquering the Italian Peninsula in a year, and becoming a national hero. In 1798, he led a military expedition to Egypt that served as a springboard to political power. He engineered a coup in November 1799 and became First Consul of the Republic.

His rising ambition and popularity inspired him to go further, and in 1804 he became the first Emperor of the French. Intractable differences with the British meant that the French were facing a Third Coalition by 1805. Napoleon shattered this coalition with decisive victories in the Ulm Campaign and a historic triumph at the Battle of Austerlitz, which led to the elimination of the Holy Roman Empire. In 1806, the Fourth Coalition took up arms against him because Prussia became worried about growing French influence on the continent. Napoleon quickly knocked out Prussia at the battles of Jena and Auerstedt, then marched the Grand Army deep into Eastern Europe, annihilating the Russians in June 1807 at Fried-land and forcing the defeated nations of the Fourth Coalition to accept the Treaties of Tilsit.

Although Tilsit signified the high watermark of the French Empire, it did not bring a lasting peace to the continent. Two years later, the Austrians challenged the French again during the War of the Fifth Coalition, but Napoleon solidified his grip over Europe after triumphing at the Battle of Wagram in July 1809. Hoping to extend the Continental System meant to choke off British goods from the European mainland, Napoleon invaded Iberia and declared his brother Joseph the King of Spain in 1808. The Spanish and the Portuguese revolted with British sup-port. The Peninsular War lasted six years, featured brutal guerrilla warfare, and culminated in victory by the allied powers of Portugal, Spain, and Britain. The Continental System caused recurring diplomatic conflicts between France and its allies, especially Russia. Unwilling to bear the economic consequences of reduced trade, the Russians violated the Continental System and enticed Napoleon into war. The French launched an invasion of Russia in the summer of 1812.

The resulting campaign witnessed the catastrophic collapse of the Grand Army, the widespread destruction of Russian lands and cities, and inspired a renewed push against Napoleon by his enemies. In 1813, Prussia and Austria joined Russian forces in a Sixth Coalition against France. A chaotic military campaign culminated in a large Allied army defeating Napoleon at the Battle of Leipzig in October 1813. The Allies then invaded France and captured Paris in the spring of 1814, forcing Napoleon to abdicate in April. He was exiled to the island of Elba near Rome and the Bourbons were restored to power.

However, Napoleon escaped from Elba in February 1815 and took control of France once again. The Allies responded by forming a Seventh Coalition, which ultimately defeated Napoleon at the Battle of Waterloo in June. The British later exiled him to the remote island of Saint Helena in the South Atlantic, where he spent the remainder of his years. His death in 1821 at the age of 51 was received with shock and grief throughout Europe.

Key Lessons

Victory Belongs To The Most Persevering.

The person who pushes through adversity is the person with the best chance of achieving their goals. Periods of difficulty teach us many lessons, the most important of these being the principle of continued testing. Without trial and error, nothing of note is gained. Adversity provides us with purpose and concentration, which focus the mind. Perseverance through adversity also teaches us the importance of responsibility, rather than the assumption of rights, which is a crucial component of success. The gained experiences of taking control of our destiny contribute to the principles that shape a noteworthy character. A fine example of perseverance is that of Thomas Edison who strode through a lengthy period of failure to eventually create the electric light bulb. His dream of illuminating a room with electricity kept his search for the correct filament for handling an electric current his dedicated priority. As Edison said, "Genius is one percent inspiration, 99 percent perspiration". The lesson we can take from Edison and Napoleon is to never give up. Whatever difficulties you encounter along the route, taking you towards your dreams, need be faced and overcome. Fear is an enemy of perseverance but this wall of anxiety must be smashed in order to achieve your goal and to experience that joyful sense of accomplishment, once the victory Napoleon mentions has been gained.

Imagination Rules The World.

Our imagination shapes how we interact with the world around us. If our mental images are full of negativity and fear we become anxious, passive, and frustrated. On the other hand, if we engage in positive thinking and imagery, our personalities are shaped to be more receptive to the good things in life. Humankind has achieved remarkable feats of creativity using the power of the imagination. A man can overcome incredible odds if he has developed his mind to see the benefits in each scenario he encounters. However, another man accustomed to defeatism and a poor self-image will instead remain stagnated, in a similar situation.

Harness the power of your imagination to cultivate positive mental images about yourself and the things you want to accomplish in life. Visualize the end-result and conjure up the emotions you believe you will feel when achieving your goal. Your imagination is now set to rule your world for the better.

Don't Be Too Cautious.

Avoiding a situation or task may feel like a sensible action to take at a particular point in time, but can actually be the most risky or damaging decision you make. According to psychologist Daniel Kanheman, our brains have developed to be risk-averse which leaves us nearly twice as sensitive to potential failures as successes. Our over-precaution stems from fear, which is wired into our brain as a protective mechanism for dealing with danger. However, when left uncontrolled and to its own devices, fear can infiltrate into every part of our lives.

This fear then reduces our ability to asses risk in an accurate manner and pre-vents us from taking actions which might improve our security and standing. The tendency of humans to underestimate the negative results of inaction was explained by the Parmenides Fallacy which occurs when one tries to assess a future state of affairs by measuring it against the present, as opposed to comparing it to other possible futures, which can frequently lead to inertia.

It's always better to take action of some kind than no action at all even if the result is not the one you intended. The 'torment of precautions' Napoleon de-scribed include symptoms such as shyness, timidity, self-consciousness, nervous-ness, guilt and above all, frustration. In order to cast off these frustrations and move through the inaction, one has to quite literally abandon one's fears and let destiny fall where it will, whilst continuing in a forward momentum.

Impossible Is An Opinion, Not A Fact.

A great many people unwittingly set themselves up for continued failure by holding negative attitudes, as touched upon previously, and habitually picturing a lack of success in their imaginations. These thinking patterns have often developed over many years and their roots can be seen in childhood. Without realizing it, these people doom themselves to mediocrity and fulfillment purely by the thoughts they entertain in their minds.

General Eisenhower once said, when asked what would have happened if the Allies had been thrown back into the sea when invading Mussolini's Italy, "it would have been very bad, but I never allowed my mind to think that way". This mind-set is typical of all successful people. Holding onto the concept of "I can't" before having even attempted a course of action, without any evidence to the contrary, is highly irrational. This is a recipe for inaction and failure. It is vital to move forward in a positive manner using the best of your abilities and knowledge whilst letting the results take care of themselves. The fact that our dreams become impossibilities in our minds before anywhere else is important to remember.

Be Where You Are Needed, And Lead Your People There

Being present is already expected from a leader; but being present where you are needed is more important. Napoleon had many people with large amounts of abilities, skills and talents under his command, and he skillfully led them where their skills are needed or required. He made it a point to be there with them, so he could direct them better. He knew where to spot opportunities where his people's skills and abilities will be put to use, and that is where he took them. The battlefield was his domain, and that was where you will find him, alongside and in front of his men. Napoleon was a very effective motivator. Wartime is definitely not a time for upbeat spirits, but with several speeches, he was able to revive the fighting spirit of men who were battle-weary and have been facing the poorest of conditions as they were led by a succession of incompetent leaders and commanders.

Be The First To Do Something.

Being a leader means having the willingness to get your hands dirty. For Napoleon, no job was beneath him. Even when he was a celebrated general, he had no qualms about getting down from his steed and getting into the trenches. He participated in the work of those that he led. This ensured that he was kept aware of what goes on in the lower ranks even when he was already up there.

For a while, the pictures painted of the quintessential leader was one that sits behind a desk (or on his throne), barking and giving orders to his subjects or servants, expecting them to buckle down and do what he told them at that very moment. This easily makes for a divisive relationship, one where the followers would have no respect for their leader, and doing something because they are told to do so, without them even wanting to do it. Being hands-on is something that employees are bound to appreciate from their leader. It tells a lot about the character of a leader when he attempts to work side by side with the people he leads. It is easier for both sides to connect and collaborate, and therefore finish the task at hand effectively and efficiently.

Say What You Mean And Mean What You Say.

Empty promises are not what you would hear from a good leader. Giving false hopes, on the other hand, is the same thing. Napoleon advocated delivering on what has been promised and by this was great at expectation management. This effectively inspired confidence and trust in his people, so they were willing to follow him wherever he led. It is important for your people – and for everyone else – to see your sincerity as a leader, and by choosing your words carefully, you can show that you mean business.

Acknowledge That You Cannot Do Everything By Yourself.

There is a general misconception that a leader must be able to do everything alone. That certainly defeats the purpose of leading a group. You need help? Then ask for it. Napoleon, no matter how accomplished a soldier and tactician he was, could not have won battles if he were alone in the charge. He needed help from others, and he was not above lowering himself and doing things for others in order to ask for it. In the end, he was able to accomplish what he set out to do.

There is one other thing that Napoleon made a point of, particularly after getting help from others: he thanked them. Whether it was through saying the words out loud, paying his soldiers with gold and silver that he has obtained, or even taking his own medal and pinning it on the coat of one his soldiers, he never failed to thank those who contributed to the cause.

Gratitude is something that is often overlooked, even in corporate settings. There is this common perception that, since everyone in business is out to get something from others (e.g. win a deal, earn profits), then it's mainly a give-and-take relationship, so saying thank you is not really all that important.

You should give credit to where, when, and to whom it is due. The modern leader who wants to follow Napoleon's example should set up an appreciation and reward system in place. It is to show his people that he appreciates the hard work they put in, and reward them for a job well done. This is a very positive way to boost their morale and motivate them to do better. On the other hand, employees who feel unappreciated and unrewarded by their leaders tend to feel disgruntled and completely unmotivated to go to work, or even think of ways to be less productive.

Be Different.

As a leader, you have to set yourself apart from your people. The greatest leaders did this by accomplishing great feats and tasks, by doing any of the following: Doing things differently. Breaking conventions and defying expectations was some-thing that Napoleon did during his time. That's what made him such a brilliant strategist, because he was not afraid to try something different, something new. Napoleon refused to stick to what was the norm, even in the way he and his men fought. As long as he saw an advantageous position for his troops, he seized it. He came up with tricks on battle formations that even bewildered his generals, but they turned out to be excellent moves, as evidenced by his victory during the Battle of the Pyramids in Egypt, when his 20,000-strong French army systematically defeated the Mamluk warriors, who had 60,000 men. As a leader, you have to al-ways be on the lookout for other, newer, ways to perform a task. It's not really a good idea to stick to only one method of dealing with one situation, especially in a competitive environment such as business, where there are competitors at every turn. By doing things in the same way over and over again, you are in danger of being predictable, so they will be able to anticipate your moves better, and you lose any advantage you may have over them.

Doing the impossible. Napoleon was seen as braver than most people, going where others would not dare, doing what others deemed impossible.

Just like in the example stated above, which could only be described by many as an impossible task. Being short of 40,000 men compared to the enemy would have been enough to make other commanders cower, but not Napoleon. Instead, he looked for ways to even up the numbers without seeking reinforcements, and that was through his brilliant strategizing.

Respect People.

Respect asks for respect. It is something that is earned, yes, even by leaders. Napoleon was able to command the respect of his soldiers by showing that he, too, had respect for them and their abilities and contributions. It did not even matter that it was the lowest-ranked foot soldier, Napoleon respected them as human beings and part of the troops, and not solely for their position in the hierarchy. Napoleon was able to build an unstoppable army, mainly because of the devotion and loyalty that he was able to instill in his soldiers. But take note that Napoleon did not just earn the devotion of his people to him, per se, but he also made sure that his people became devoted to their cause. He made them want victory and glory in every battle as much as he did.

Know Your People And Understand Them.

This is also another way of showing that you respect your people: get to know them and understand how they feel. Napoleon also took this as an opportunity to predict outcomes, especially when faced with unexpected circumstances or situations. Planning and strategizing became easier because Napoleon knew his people, so he knew where to put resources in the field.

Do Not Silence Your People.

Let them speak their minds and say their peace. Do not just hear them out; re-ally listen to what they say. Get their thoughts, ideas, and opinions; you will be surprised at how much you can learn just by letting your people talk and by listening to what they have to say. Putting restrictions or limitations on them will also potentially be limiting to your effectiveness as a leader, and of your group's goals. More importantly, pay attention to what your people think about how you are as a leader. After all, they are in the best position to say whether you are going a good job leading them or not.

Trust Your People.

This is probably one of the hardest things for a leader (for anyone, really) to do but, by trusting your people, you are also working towards getting them to trust you. People find it easier to give their loyalty and trust to someone who shows that they trust them back. In the Battle of the Pyramids, for example, Napoleon trusted that his men will come through, despite being outnumbered. In return, his men trusted him to come up with a strategy for them to survive and beat the enemies.

Look People In The Eye.

It's a very simple thing to do, yet not a lot of people manage to do it. It's called eye contact, and it is a quality that every good leader should have. By looking at another person straight in their eye, you are acknowledging their existence and showing that you are listening to what they have to say. It also serves as one way to gauge the person you are talking to. Sizing up a rival or an enemy will be easier when you look into their eyes, since it has been said all too often that the eyes are the windows of one's soul. You can tell a lot about a person by watching how their eyes move, shift, or react.

Control Your Temper.

More often than not, we are our own worst enemy, and anger is not going to help any. Anger is one sure way to cloud one's judgment and, as a good leader, you are not supposed to let go of the clarity of your judgment. By managing his anger, Napoleon was able to keep his emotions in check and keep a clear head on the battlefield, where every decision – even the smallest one – could make the difference between life and death.

Do Not Speak In Anger.

People who let anger rule over them tend to say things that they soon regret later on. In the process, they hurt other people, and they also lose the respect that those people had for them. The key is to not make decisions when you are feeling emotional. Unless you have a handle on your emotions, do not decide on anything. Deliberation requires a level head, and being emotional – not just plain furious – won't let you do that objectively.

Have Respect For Your Time.

You might not know it, but you might be disrespecting the time that is available to you by doing things that are irrelevant and will not really give you any satisfaction. Napoleon showed great efficiency in managing time and becoming an excel-lent organizer. This was also apparent in how Napoleon was known to focus on the key issues at hand. With so many issues to sort through, he knew which points to pay attention to, and which ones can be ignored or left for another day.

You often hear businessmen say that "time is money", and there is a lot of truth to this. Time wasted means money wasted in business, which is why business leaders should make sure they manage their time well. The Pomodoro technique is great for managing your time.

Never Stop Learning.

A leader should never feel and act like he knows everything and, thus, no longer sees the need to learn anything more. There is always, ALWAYS, some-thing new to learn. Napoleon never stopped seeking to improve himself by acquiring knowledge and learning whatever could be learned, which he then used in his future endeavors. Even as a young boy, he read a lot, focusing on the Classics, particularly those of notable leaders in history such as Alexander the Great.

In the formulation of the Napoleonic Code, Napoleon entrusted the task to equally brilliant individuals, but he still joined the lengthy meetings, astounding everyone with his amazing grasp of all the relevant details. This is proof that, even at the height of his power as a leader, he never stopped learning. Leaders in business have to be aware of a lot of things, even beyond the scope of the industry that they are in. This is not just a way to widen their horizons, but to also keep their minds alert and sharp, to make it easier for them to spot opportunities once they arise.

Napoleon was unquestionably a great strategist and imposing historical figure.

His leadership style had many flaws, which eventually led to his downfall.

Never Stop Innovating.

Napoleon introduced many tactical innovations to warfare and statecraft. He believed in lightning military attacks when most European generals were slow, in-competent or incapable of making on-the-ground decisions without higher orders. He struck fear in the hearts of his opponents by bombarding them with canon and grapeshot believing, correctly, that loud noises shook the nerve of his opponents. And he was one of the first leaders to wield propaganda to bolster his position at home and abroad. But Napoleon never improved on his basic innovations. He never cared to learn about naval weapons, steam power, observation balloons, rail-roads, bridging materials, troop ships and general advances in canon ammunition.

Napoleon never bothered to think about France's large land holding in Amer-ica. He feared crossing the Atlantic and instead of finding a use for the vast terri-tory, he sold it. Paul Johnson in his biography of Napoleon, writes, "He thought the improvements introduced in his youth were quite enough, and though he fid-dled with the standard equipment, he never changed it substantially." Napoleon's failure to adapt eventually hurt his military and political campaigns in the long run. By failing to build a navy and look to alternative innovations and business deals he lost his ability to outmaneuver his opponents and with it his edge. Old tricks may work over and over again, but never overlook new technologies. Over-time they will become crucial.

Learn To Delegate.

Napoleon's subordinates could pull off miracles, but only when under strict, careful instruction. Those high in Napoleon's favor were those who obeyed orders precisely. Promotions weren't given to those who had independent ideas. The result: when Napoleon's generals had to think on their own or perform without Napoleon's instruction, they were often nervous, fumbling and counterproductive.

Leaders shouldn't simply promote those who can follow orders. Empower employees to think for themselves and they'll do better under pressure, even without orders.

Have A Little Patience.

There are many battles Napoleon could have won if he had been more patient. He might have also attained more power if he had grown more organically, rather than rushing, impulsively into Spain and Russia." Bonaparte lacked the temperament to fight a defensive battle, let alone a defensive campaign," writes Johnson. "Had he been able to do so, he might well have fought the Sixth Coalition to a peace of exhaustion, without a single one of its soldiers setting foot on French soil proper." Focusing all your energy on forward movement might seem like the right thing to do, especially if it's what has led to your success before. However, every leader needs to be expert in controlling active periods as well as calm ones.

Take Training Seriously.

Napoleon selected 50,000 men to serve in his elite, Old Guard. They were tall, strong, standout soldiers who wore menacing bearskin uniforms. During battle they would sit behind the main forces and their presence would give the regular troops confidence. However, Napoleon rarely had to call on the Old Guard's services since he usually won battles quickly and with skill. But his success would eventually backfire. When Napoleon finally needed to call on the Old Guard during the battle of Waterloo they were weak, unused to fighting and underprepared. Don't set aside high-potential employees and keep them above the fray. Leaders need to ensure their teams are well trained in all tasks and don't lose their relevance.

Don't Lose Your Temper.

Napoleon had a bad temper. Sometimes he'd fly off the handle over small matters and sometimes he'd plan a fit hoping that his dramatics would inspire his subordinates to action. He used his loud outbursts to inspire fear and respect in the ranks, but they rarely won him points in diplomatic circles. When Napoleon met with the British ambassador Lord Whitworth, he threw a fit then stalked out of the room so quickly that the doormen hadn't time to open the doors. Napoleon had to wait, seething, until the doors were opened. Such hysterics made Napoleon look uncertain, weak and hotheaded.

Control your temper. Outbursts have very limited mileage and, more often than not, make you look foolish.

CHAPTER 9

LUCIUS SERGIUS

CATILINA

Lucius Sergius Catilina, known in English, as Catiline is an aristocrat who turned demagogue and made an unsuccessful attempt to overthrow the republic while Cicero was a consul. Catiline served under Pompey's father in the Social War of 89 and acquired an unsavory reputation as a zealous participant in Sulla's proscriptions, killing his own brother-in-law during them. He was acquitted of charges of fornication with a Vestal Virgin in 73 and afterward became praetor in 68 and governor of the province of Africa in 67–66. Because Catiline was then under prosecution for extortion, a charge of which he was eventually acquitted, he could not stand for the consular elections of 65 or 64.

Later there was talk that he had planned to murder the consuls and seize power early in 65, but there is no solid evidence for this "first Catilinarian conspiracy." In 64 Catiline failed to be elected consul when Cicero was one of the successful candidates, and a year later he was again defeated for that office. Upon this last defeat, Catiline began to systematically enlist a body of supporters with which to stage an armed insurrection and seizes control of the government. His proposals for the cancellation of debt and the proscription of wealthy citizens and his general championship of the poor and oppressed appealed to a variety of discontented elements within Roman society: victims of Sulla's proscriptions who had been dispossessed of their property, veterans of Sulla's forces who had failed to succeed as farmers on the land awarded to them, opportunists and desperadoes, and aristocratic malcontents.

Cicero, who was consul in 63, was kept fully informed of the growing conspiracy by his network of spies and informers, but he felt unable to act against the still-popular and well-connected Catiline. On October 21, however, Cicero denounced Catiline to the Senate in an impassioned speech, charging him with treason and obtaining from the Senate the "ultimate decree," in effect a proclamation of martial law. Catiline withdrew from Rome on November 8 and joined his army of destitute veterans and other supporters that had been collected at Faesulae in Etruria. Despite these events, the Senate remained only partly convinced of the immediate danger that Catiline represented.

On December 3, however, some envoys of the Gallic tribe of the Allobroges, whose support had been imprudently solicited by important Catilinarian conspirators in Rome, provided Cicero with a number of signed documents that unmistakably proved the conspiracy's existence. These suspects were arrested by Cicero and were executed on December 5 by decree of the now-thoroughly alarmed Senate. The Senate also mobilized the republic's armies to take the field against Catiline's forces. Catiline, assuming charge of the army at Faesulae, attempted to cross the Apennines into Gaul in January but was engaged by a republican army under Gaius Antonius Hybrida at Pistoria. Fighting bravely against great odds, Catiline and most of his followers were killed. Catiline was found, far in advance of his men, among the dead bodies of the enemy; a most glorious death, had he thus fallen for his country.

After Catiline's death, many of the poor still regarded him with respect and did not view him as the traitor and villain that Cicero claimed he was. However, the aristocratic element of Rome certainly viewed him in a much darker light. Sallust wrote an account of the conspiracy that epitomized Catiline as representative of all of the evils festering in the declining Roman republic. In his account, Sallust at-tributes countless crimes and atrocities to Catiline, but even he refuses to heap some of the most outrageous claims on him, particularly a ritual that involved the drinking of blood of a sacrificed child. Later historians such as Florus and Dio Cassius, far removed from the original events, recorded the claims of Sallust and the aforementioned rumors as facts. Up until the modern era Catiline was equated, as Sallust described, to everything depraved and contrary to both the laws of the gods and men.

Nevertheless, many Romans still viewed his character with a degree of respect. Well after Catiline's death and the end of the threat of the conspiracy, even Cicero reluctantly admitted that Catiline was an enigmatic man who possessed both the greatest of virtues and the most terrible of vices. He had many things about him which served to allure men to the gratification of their passions; he had also many things which acted as incentives to industry and toil. The vices of lust raged in him; but at the same time he was conspicuous for great energy and military skill. Nor do I believe that there ever existed so strange a prodigy upon the earth, made up in such a manner of the most various, and different and inconsistent studies and desires.

Catiline spoke with an eloquence that demanded loyalty from his followers and strengthened the resolve of his friends. Without doubt Catiline possessed a degree of courage that few have, and he died a particularly honorable death in Roman so-ciety. Unlike most Roman generals of the late republic, Catiline offered himself to his followers both as a general and as soldier on the front lines. While history has viewed Catiline through the lenses of his enemies, some modern historians have reassessed Catiline, such as Michael Parenti, in "The Assassination of Julius Caesar".

To some extent Catiline's name has been freed from many of its previous associations, and even to some the name of Catiline has undergone a transformation from a traitor and villain to a heroic agrarian reformer. Thus, some view Catiline as a reformer such as the Gracchi who met similar resistance from the government. However, many place him somewhere in between, a man who used the plight of the poor to suit his personal interests and a politician of the time no more corrupt than any other. Interestingly in parts of Italy up until the Middle Ages the legend of 'Catellina' continued to exist and was favorable to him.

Still other scholarly texts, such as H. E. Gould and J. L. Whiteley's Macmillan edition of Cicero's In Catilinam, dismiss Catiline as a slightly deranged revolutionary, concerned more with the cancellation of his own debts, accrued in running for so many consulships, and in achieving the status he believed his by birthright due to his family name.

Key Lessons:

Ruthless Focus, Relentless Execution

Voltaire said, "No problem can withstand the assault of sustained thinking." It's true. Likewise, no challenge can withstand our sustained action. When it comes to making things happen on a consistent basis, no single strategy has served me better than extreme focus and relentless execution. Act on your best idea, in some small way. Over time, with sustained focus, relentless thinking, and little actions, you compound your effort into greater results. Keep in mind, that sometimes the best way to get great results is to take massive action. In the words of Dan Brown, "Everything is possible. The impossible just takes longer."

Choose Your Response

"All change happens with a choice." — Tony Robbins

Don't let other people push your buttons. Expand the space between the stimulus and the response.

Stephen Covey said it best:

"In the space between stimulus (what happens) and how we respond, lies our freedom to choose. Ultimately, this power to choose is what defines us as human beings. We may have limited choices but we can always choose. We can choose our thoughts, emotions, moods, our words, our actions; we can choose our values and live by principles. It is the choice of acting or being acted upon."

As one of my mentors puts it, "You are the sum of your decisions."

Exercise your choices. When it comes to making big change and making big choices, put yourself into a position where failure is not an option. Tony Robbins shares this advice:

"If you want to take the island – burn the friggin' boats!"

Enjoy The Journey And The Destination

""Life is like skiing. Just like skiing, the goal is not to get to the bottom of the hill. It's to have a bunch of good runs before the sun sets." – Seth Godin

It's one thing to focus on your destination. It's another to enjoy the journey as you go. Do both. Find a way to make the journey worth it. Sometimes, you won't actually reach your destination. You'll want to look back and know that you made your journey worth it, you stopped to smell the flowers along the way, and if you had to do it all over again, there's a good chance you'd do it the same way.

Be Here Now

Be here now. Your choices are in the moment. You can choose what you focus on. You choose whether to worry or take. action. Now is a great time to act. Right here, right now, you can think the thoughts that serve you. Throughout the day, you'll have learning opportunities and leadership moments. In the moments throughout the day, you can connect what you do and how you do it back to your values. In this moment, do you know what you want, what you think, and what you feel?

CHAPTER 10

NAPOLEON III

Napoleon III, was the Emperor (1852–70) of the Second French Empire. He was the nephew and heir of Napoleon I. He was the first President of France to be elected by a direct popular vote. He was blocked by the Constitution and Parliament from running for a second term, so he organized a coup d'état in 1851 and then took the throne as Napoleon III on 2 December 1852, the forty-eighth anniversary of Napoleon I's coronation. He remains the longest-serving French head of state since the French Revolution. During the first years of the Empire, Napoleon's government imposed censorship and harsh repressive measures against his opponents. Some six thousand were imprisoned or sent to penal colonies until 1859. Thousands more went into voluntary exile abroad, including Victor Hugo.

From 1862 onwards, he relaxed government censorship, and his regime came to be known as the "Liberal Empire." Many of his opponents returned to France and became members of the National Assembly. Napoleon III is best known today for his grand reconstruction of Paris, carried out by his prefect of the Seine Baron Haussmann. He launched similar public works projects in Marseille, Lyon, and other French cities. Napoleon III modernized the French banking system, greatly expanded and consolidated the French railway system, and made the French mer-chant marine the second largest in the world.

He promoted the building of the Suez Canal and established modern agriculture, which ended famines in France and made France an agricultural exporter. He negotiated the 1860 Cobden–Chevalier free trade agreement with Britain and similar agreements with France's other European trading partners. Social reforms included giving French workers the right to strike and the right to organize. Women's education greatly expanded, as did the list of required subjects in public schools.

In foreign policy, Napoleon III aimed to reassert French influence in Europe and around the world. He was a supporter of popular sovereignty and of nationalism. In Europe, he allied with Britain and defeated Russia in the Crimean War (1853–56). His regime assisted Italian unification and, in doing so, annexed Savoy and the County of Nice to France; at the same time, his forces de-fended the Papal States against annexation by Italy. Napoleon doubled the area of the French overseas empire in Asia, the Pacific, and Africa. On the other hand, his army's intervention in Mexico aimed to create a Second Mexican Empire under French protection but ended in failure.

Beginning in 1866, Napoleon had to face the mounting power of Prussia, as Chancellor Otto von Bismarck sought German unification under Prussian leader-ship. In July 1870, Napoleon entered the Franco-Prussian War without allies and with inferior military forces. The French army was rapidly defeated and Napoleon III. was captured at the Battle of Sedan. The French Third Republic was pro claimed in Paris, and Napoleon went into exile in England, where he died in 1873.

Born in 1808 in Paris, France, Napoleon III, the nephew of Napoleon I, grew up in exile—the year 1815 marked the end of Napoleon I's reign. However, Napoleon III was determined to regain the French throne. He began his quest in 1832, writing various political and military tracts in an effort to make himself and his ideas known. After a failed coup attempt in 1836, he was exiled again. After the Revolution of 1848, in 1850, Napoleon III was elected president of the Second Republic. He served in that position until 1852, when he was made emperor—a position he held until 1870, when the disastrous Franco-Prussian War led to his capture. He was deposed and sent to England, where he died in 1873.

Key Lessons:

Cultivate An Attitude Of Gratitude

"Happiness is not having what you want, but wanting what you have." — Rabbi H Schachtel

Acknowledgement and appreciation are the most powerful rewards on Earth. You can cultivate your attitude of gratitude by being thankful for the good choices you make during your day. Acknowledge and appreciate when you make the tough call, do the right thing, or take the high road.

Tony Robbins starts his day from a place of strength by reminding himself what he's grateful for. Whenever you can't find a way to be grateful for what you've got, remind yourself how things can always be worse, and if you look for examples, you'll find plenty. There is always somebody worse off than you.

Create a Feedback Loop

"Feedback is the breakfast of champions." — Ken Blanchard

The fastest way to improve with skill is to get a feedback loop that gives you data to learn and improve from. Find ways to build learning loops, where you can iterate on something, and get a little better each time. If you're not getting the in-sight you need, fast enough, or relevant enough, then tighten your loop.

Form a Personal Board of Directors

Find people in your life that you trust to give you deep feedback on ways to improve. They may even know you better than you know yourself. Find the people and friends who are willing to offer you insight and guidance on how to bring out your best.

Give Your Best Where You've Got Your Best to Give

Spend more time in your strengths. It's one thing to play to your strengths when you get the chance. It's another thing to deliberately find ways to spend a lot more time in your strengths. John Wooden's secret to a happy life was peace of mind. His secret to peace of mind was giving his best, every chance he got.

Stay Hands-On

Use it or lose it. Don't be afraid to roll up your sleeves and dive in. It's part of learning. When I was at Tiffany & Co, the head of our department always reminded us that you learn more by doing, and that you're never above any job. And he would add that the more you know about the job at all levels, the more capable you are as you go up.

Surround Yourself with Catalysts

Robin Hood had his Merry Men. Build your wolf pack. Some people we know, just happen to bring out our best. Somehow, when you're around them, you smile a little more.

You feel a little stronger. You walk a little taller. You shine a little brighter. They are your catalysts. Surround yourself with the people that lift you.

Embrace Change

"It is not the strongest of the species that survive, nor the most intelligent, but the one most responsive to change." — Charles Darwin

Change is a constant in our lives. If we embrace it, we can use it as an opportunity to let go of what's not working, and carry forward what is. We can also use it to reinvent ourselves.

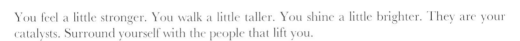

CHAPTER 11

ANGELA ISADORA

DUNC

Isadora Duncan (1877-1927) was an American pioneer of dance and is an important figure in both the arts and history. Known as the "Mother of Modern Dance," Isadora Duncan was a self-styled revolutionary whose influence spread from American to Europe and Russia, creating a sensation everywhere she per-formed. Her style of dancing eschewed the rigidity of ballet and she championed the notion of free-spiritedness coupled with the high ideals of ancient Greece: beauty, philosophy, and humanity. She brought into being a totally new way to dance, and it is this unique gift of Isadora Duncan that the Isadora Duncan Dance Foundation wishes to preserve, present, and protect.

Dancer, adventurer, and ardent defender of the free spirit, Isadora Duncan is one of the most enduring influences on contemporary culture and can be credited with inventing what came to be known as Modern Dance. With free-flowing costumes, bare feet, and loose hair, she took to the stage inspired by the ancient Greeks, the music of classical composers, the wind and the sea. Isadora elevated the dance to a high place among the arts, returning the discipline to its roots as a sacred art. Duncan shed the restrictive corsets of the Victorian era and broke away from the vocabulary of the ballet. Stepping out of the dance studio with a vi-sion of the dance of the future, Isadora embraced artists, philosophers, and writ-ers as her teachers and guides.

According to Isadora, the development of her dance was a natural phenomenon – not an invention, but a rediscovery of the classical principles of beauty, motion, and form. Her dances were born of the impulse to embrace life's bittersweet challenges, meeting destiny and fate head-on in her own whirlwind journey, filled with both tragedy and ecstasy. She was determined to "dance a different dance," telling her own life story through abstract, universal expressions of the human condition.

Shocking some audience members and inspiring others, Isadora posed a challenge to the prevailing orthodoxies of her time. Isadora was a champion in the struggle for women's rights. Many saw a glorious vision for the future in Isadora's choreography. Her influence upon the development of progressive ideas and culture from her time to our own has yet to be measured. She has inspired artists, thinkers, and idealists everywhere.

Isadora Duncan was born in San Francisco, California on May 26, 1877, the youngest of four. Her parents were divorced by 1880 and her mother Dora moved with her children to Oakland, where she struggled to make ends meet as a piano teacher. Mrs. Duncan spent her evenings reading aloud to her "Clan Duncan", the works of Shakespeare, Browning, Shelley, Keats, Dickens, Ingersoll and Whit-man; sowing the seeds of artistic inspiration in her youngest child, Isadora. In her
early years, Isadora attended school but found it stifling and dropped out at the age of ten to be self-educated at the Oakland public library under the guidance of poet-laureate Ina Coolbrith. Ever resourceful, Isadora and her sister Elizabeth earned extra money by teaching dance classes to local children. After a series of ballet lessons at age 9, Isadora proclaimed ballet a school of "affected grace and toe walking," and quit. Later, in her autobiography My Life, Isadora wrote that in her opinion, ballet training resulted in the look and feel of an "articulated pup-pet…producing artificial mechanical movement not worthy of the soul."

In 1895, with a voracious appetite for art and life, Isadora traveled first to Chicago, and then to New York and by 1899 she moved to Europe to continue developing her art.

During her youth in San Francisco, Isadora had already formulated her signature movement style. As she matured, she developed her choreography and started setting her dances to early Italian music, with costumes and dance mo-tifs inspired by Renaissance paintings and ancient Greek myths. As a "California novelty" Duncan was invited to perform for salons and garden parties by wealthy patrons of the arts. She was often met with opposition and ridicule. One society lady is known to have remarked, "If my daughter dressed like Miss Duncan I would lock her up in the attic!" Isadora struggled financially but rejected invitations to perform in vaudeville circuit variety shows.

Eventually, this original and intrepid Californian caught the attention of the Hungarian press. In 1902 her debut performances in Budapest with a full orchestra were a critical success and ran sold-out for 30 days. Her encore was Johann Strauss's popular and intoxicating waltz The Blue Danube.Within two years of performing her own choreography, Duncan had achieved both notoriety and success. At this point, she could afford to take her spiritual pilgrimage to Greece, realizing her life's dream to touch the sacred marble of the Acropolis and steep her-self in the ancient mysteries of Greek art and architecture.

In 1905, Isadora settled in Gruenwald outside of Berlin and opened her first dance school. She subsidized the entire establishment with proceeds from her tours. Along with her sister Elizabeth, she started training the young dancers who would become her performing company, "The Isadorables," as dubbed by the press. Initially, she enrolled twenty girls and boys, but her effort to include boys was unsuccessful and was finally dropped due to a lack of funds.

By this time, Isadora had begun to achieve celebrity status among the artistic and cultural illuminati of her day. Auguste Rodin, Michel Fokine,Vaslav Nijinsky, and Gertrude Stein all paid tribute to her in sculpture, choreography, and poetry. When the Théâtre des Champs-Élysées was constructed in 1913, Isadora's image was sculpted by Antoine Bourdelle for the facade and murals in the auditorium.

Duncan had vowed never to marry, but out of wedlock, she had a daughter named Deirdre whose father was the famous set designer, Edward Gordon Craig. Although their passionate love affair ended after several years, he was to remain her lifelong friend. Her second child, Patrick, was fathered by a wealthy heir to a sewing machine fortune named Paris Singer. Singer underwrote the founding and operation of another of Duncan's second school prior to World War I in Bellevue, just outside of Paris. Later, in 1913, Deirdre and Patrick drowned with their nanny as their car rolled into the river Seine. Isadora was devastated. Her dances Mother and Marche Funebre, featuring music by Scriabin and Chopin respectively, were inspired by her loss and conveyed her heartbreak on a universal level.

Picking up the pieces, Isadora retreated to Italy to spend time with her friend Eleanora Duse, and started work on choreography set to Schubert's 9th Symphony and Tchaikovsky's 6th Symphony. Between 1916 and 1920, she performed solo and toured extensively across Europe and America, including one sojourn to South America. Isadora was greatly taken with the social and political revolution that led to the creation of the Soviet Union. Believing that she could contribute to the development of a free and heroic society, Duncan followed her conviction and passion to Moscow in 1921 to make arrangements with the new government to found a new school of dance. She longed to "give her art in exchange for a free school," and to "teach a thousand children." Operating the Moscow school with help from Irma Duncan, Isadora experienced one of her most artistically prolific and critically successful periods. Timeless and mature works including The Revolutionary with music by Scriabin and a suite of dances set to Russian work songs communicate her fury at social injustice, her empathy with human suffering, and

her faith in the power of perseverance to overcome obstacles. In Moscow, Isadora met the young poet Sergei Esenin and broke her previous vow by marrying him in order that he be allowed to travel with her during a tour of Ameri a. America de-nounced Isadora's outspoken love of Russia but Duncan was unrepentant: "Yes, I am a revolutionist," she said to the press, "All true artists are revolutionists."

Isadora Duncan's death was as dramatic as her life. On September 14, 1927, she encountered a young driver in Nice, France and suggested he take her for a spin in his open-air Bugatti sports car. As the car took off, she reportedly shouted to her friends, "Adieu, mes amis, je vais a la gloire!" — "Goodbye my friends, I go to glory!" Moments later, her trailing shawl became entangled in the rear wheel, breaking her neck instantly.

Despite Duncan's untimely death, her legacy continues to inspire contemporary artists and boundary-breaking minds around the world. Early in Isadora's career, sculptor Laredo Taft had described her as "Poetry personified. She is not the tenth muse but all nine muses in one." And so it was. There are over 40 books about Isadora Duncan, countless drawings, paintings, and sculptures, two major motion pictures, a dozen TV documentaries, and several plays and poems.

Key Lessons:

Anticipate It

"The best way to predict the future is to create it." — Peter F. Drucker

Be what's next. Think ahead. Anticipate. A lot of the same things happen every day, every week, every month, every year. Watch for the patterns. Make them work for you. You'd be surprised how many things we think are random can be traced back to a simple flow of events that weren't random at all. When you get in the habit of looking head, you set the stage to help yourself prepare for changes that may come your way, long before they start to show up.

Age Like a Fine Wine

Some people let time wear them down. Others put time on their side. They get better with age. Imagine if you got just a little better each day, how quickly that adds up over time. Imagine you a year from now, better in so many ways, through better choices, better habits, and better thoughts.

Seek Progress, Not Perfection

"The perfect is the enemy of good." – Voltaire

Perfection is a great way to paralyze yourself. Improvement over time beats seeking perfection out of the gate. Think of perfection as a journey, not a destination, and enjoy the journey as you go.

Add More Life to Your Years

"And in the end, it's not the years in your life that count. It's the life in your years." — Abraham Lincoln

Life's short. You can try to add more years to your life, but first add more life to your years. Otherwise, what's the point.

Raise Your Frustration Tolerance

Imagine if you found out that your frustration tolerance level was the main thing holding you back from enjoying life a little more each day? Think of all the little thing that bug you each day. Maybe it's the traffic. Maybe it's people you know.

Maybe it's a lot of little things throughout your day, that all seem to rub you the wrong way. Imagine if you suddenly raised your frustration tolerance, and all the little things that bugged you no longer pushed your buttons? This is one of those big choices in life that affects you every day.

Take One Step Back to Take Two Steps Forward

I remember the pain of learning to type. I thought my two-finger method was fine. I hadn't realized how much faster I could be. But getting there was painful. Speed didn't come easy. It was like taking a step back. Eventually, taking the step back paid off, and now I get the benefit on a daily basis. A lot of things you learn can be like that. Learning is awkward. But the results are worth it, if you stick with it.

Change the Things that Aren't Working for You

"Insanity: doing the same thing over and over again and expecting different results." — Albert Einstein

As Tony Robbins reminds us, "If you do what you've always done, you'll get what you've always gotten." If things aren't working for you, change them.

Change Yourself First.

The fastest person you can change in any situation is you. If you're not getting the results you want, try changing yourself first. Change your rules. It's easy to create a bunch of rules for yourself that make success impossible, or always out of reach. Change your environment. As Deepak Chopra , "You can't make positive choices for the rest of your life without an environment that makes those choices easy, natural, and enjoyable."

Change Your Relationships.

As W. Clement Stone says, "Be careful the friends you choose for you will become like them." Change your metaphors for life. Is your life a comedy? A tragedy? A sitcom? An epic adventure? A dance? Change how your represent things. Change what they mean to you. When you change how you represent things, you change how you experience them.

Ask Better Questions

If you want better answers in life, ask better questions. What are some better questions you can start asking yourself ? Exactly.

CHAPTER 12

THOMAS WOODROW WILSON

Thomas Woodrow Wilson (December 28, 1856 – February 3, 1924) was an American politician and academic who served as the 28th President of the United States from 1913 to 1921. Born in Staunton, Virginia, he spent his early years in Augusta, Georgia and Columbia, South Carolina. Wilson earned a PhD in political science at Johns Hopkins University, and served as a professor and scholar at various institutions before being chosen as President of Princeton University, a position he held from 1902 to 1910. In the election of 1910, he was the gubernatorial candidate of New Jersey's Democratic Party, and was elected the 34th Governor of New Jersey, serving from 1911 to 1913.

Running for president in 1912, Wilson benefited from a split in the Republican Party, which enabled his plurality of just over forty percent to win him a large Electoral College margin. He was the first Southerner elected as president since 1848, and Wilson was a leading force in the Progressive Movement, bolstered by his Democratic Party's winning control of both the White House and Congress in 1912.

In office, Wilson reintroduced the spoken State of the Union, which had been out of use since 1801. Leading the Congress, now in Democratic hands, he over-saw the passage of progressive legislative policies unparalleled until the New Deal in 1933. Included among these were the Federal Reserve Act, Federal Trade Com-mission Act, the Clayton Antitrust Act, and the Federal Farm Loan Act. Having taken office one month after ratification of the Sixteenth Amendment, Wilson called a special session of Congress, whose work culminated in the Revenue Act of 1913, reintroducing an income tax and lowering tariffs. Through passage of the Adamson Act, imposing an 8-hour workday for railroads, he averted a railroad strike and an ensuing economic crisis.

Upon the outbreak of World War I in 1914, Wilson maintained a policy of neutrality, while pursuing a more aggressive policy in dealing with Mexico's civil war. Wilson faced former New York Governor Charles Evans Hughes in the presidential election of 1916. By a narrow margin, he became the first Democrat since An-drew Jackson elected to two consecutive terms. Wilson's second term was dominated by American entry into World War I. In April 1917, when Germany resumed unrestricted submarine warfare, Wilson asked Congress to declare war in order to make "the world safe for democracy."

The United States conducted military operations alongside the Allies, although without a formal alliance. Also in 1917, he denied sanctuary to Tsarist Russia's Nicholas II and his immediate family when Nicholas was overthrown in that year's February Revolution and forced into abdication that March, a decision that be-came controversial the following year with the shooting of the Romanov family in 1918. During the war, Wilson focused on diplomacy and financial considerations, leaving military strategy to the generals, especially General John J. Pershing. Loan-ing billions of dollars to Britain, France, and other Allies, the United States aided their finance of the war effort. Through the Selective Service Act, conscription sent 10,000 freshly trained soldiers to France per day by the summer of 1918.

On the home front, he raised income taxes, borrowing billions of dollars through the public's purchase of Liberty Bonds. He set up the War Industries Board, promoted labor union cooperation, regulating agriculture and food production through the Lever Act, and granting to the Secretary of the Treasury, William McAdoo, direct control of the nation's railroad system.

In his 1915 State of the Union, Wilson asked Congress for what became the Espionage Act of 1917 and the Sedition Act of 1918, suppressing anti-draft activists. The crackdown was intensified by his Attorney General A. Mitchell Palmer to include expulsion of non-citizen radicals during the First Red Scare of 1919–1920. Following years of advocacy for suffrage on the state level, in 1918 he endorsed the Nineteenth Amendment, whose ratification in 1920 provided equal right to vote for women across the United States, over Southern opposition. Wilson staffed his government with Southern Democrats who believed in segregation.[4] He gave department heads greater autonomy in their management.[5] Early in 1918, he issued his principles for peace, the Fourteen Points, and in 1919, following armistice, he traveled to Paris, promoting the formation of a League of Nations, concluding the Treaty of Versailles.

Following his return from Europe, Wilson embarked on a nationwide tour in 1919 to campaign for the treaty, suffering a severe stroke. The treaty was met with serious concern by Senate Republicans, and Wilson rejected a compromise effort led by Henry Cabot Lodge, leading to the Senate's rejection of the treaty. Due to his stroke, Wilson secluded himself in the White House, disability having diminished his power and influence. Forming a strategy for reelection, Wilson dead-locked the 1920 Democratic National Convention, but his bid for a third-term nomination was overlooked.

A devoted Presbyterian, Wilson infused morality into his internationalism, an ideology now referred to as "Wilsonian"—an activist foreign policy calling on the nation to promote global democracy. For his sponsorship of the League of Nations, Wilson was awarded the 1919 Nobel Peace Prize, the second of three sitting presidents so honored.

Woodrow Wilson left the White House broken physically but serenely confident that his vision of America playing a central role in a league of nations would be realized eventually. While it can be argued that his stubbornness or his physical col-lapse prevented his realizing the dream that was within his grasp in 1919, there can be no doubt that his ideal inspired many Americans and that it shaped much of American foreign policy for the remainder of the twentieth century.

Despite the tragedy of his last year in office, Wilson left an enduring legacy. His transformation of the basic objective of American foreign policy from isolation to internationalism, his success in making the Democratic Party a "party of reform," and his ability to shape and mobilize public opinion fashioned the modern presidency. Under his leadership, Congress enacted the most cohesive, complete, and elaborate program of federal oversight of the nation's economy up to that time: banking reform under the auspices of the Federal Reserve System, tariff reduction, federal regulation of business, support for labor and collective bargaining, and federal aid to education and agriculture.

Together, these programs helped the United States begin to catch up with what was happening in other industrial states around the world. They reflected a deep commitment to humanization of the industrial system and laid the basis for the modern welfare state. His wartime mobilization program became a model for the New Deal's fight against the Great Depression in the 1930s and for Franklin Roosevelt's mobilization policies during World War II. He was the first statesman of world stature to speak out not only against European imperialism but against the newer form of economic domination sometimes described as "informal imperial-ism." For repressed ethnic and national groups around the world, his call for "national self-determination" was the herald's trumpet for a new era.

Domestically, he was perhaps the most important transitional figure among the Presidents since Lincoln. Theodore Roosevelt, while redefining the modern president as a steward of the common good of the nation, continued the progressive tradition long associated with the party of Lincoln. Wilson took a party mired in southern conservatism and big-city machine politics that had resisted William Jennings Bryan's reform proposals and made its basic agenda progressive. With his presidency, the Democratic Party assumed the mantle of reform while Republicans became more conservative. On the negative side, Wilson's idealism some-times led to him astray.

If his commitment to self-determination led him to set the Philippines on the road to independence, in Latin America, his desire to promote the benefits of democracy produced the invasion and military occupation of Haiti and the Dominican Republic. And if he generally avoided those mistakes in Mexico, it is hard not to suspect that major reasons for his restraint were the practical problems associated with imposing a regime on that large nation. He tolerated no dissent during the war and authorized serious violations of Americans' civil liberties in his quest for victory. Nor did his zest for humanitarian justice extend to American blacks: He accepted segregation in government departments and did little to stop the waves of anti-Black violence and race riots that swept over the land during his ad-ministration, particularly in the years after the war—although, to be fair, it must be noted that his illness during this period kept him ignorant of much of what was happening.

During the period of neutrality prior to American entrance into World War I, Wilson could have avoided conflict with Germany by restricting Americans' travel into the war zone, but his stubborn insistence that German submarines must re-spect the lives and property of neutrals upheld the ideals of international law while ignoring the reality that technology had transformed warfare. Moreover, his principled rejection of using the threat of an arms embargo to blackmail the British into modifying their restrictions on American trade frustrated and infuriated the Germans, thus increasing the risk of war with the United States. In these cases, idealism carried a substantial cost.

Critics claim that Wilson went to war at least partly to resist the spread of communism and to hasten U.S. economic penetration of world markets. Although Wilson described the postwar treatment of Russia, in his Fourteen Points speech, as the "acid test" of the peace treaty, he agreed to exclude the Russians from the peace conference. Some critics see that decision and his sending 15,000 American soldiers into Russia in 1918 as evidence of his hostility to communism and his aggressive desire to overthrow the Bolshevik government in order to make the world safe for American capitalism. For such historians, Wilson's action, when seen in the context of the Palmer Raids and his heavy-handed treatment of socialists at home, was a principal cause of the Cold War.

When legacy is defined as influence on the nation and future politics, Wilson ranks with Washington, Lincoln, and Franklin Roosevelt in importance. Richard Nixon recognized the power of Wilson's legacy when he returned Wilson's desk to the Oval Office in 1969. Nixon saw himself as the President who would establish a new, Wilsonian world order of stability and collective security to replace the Cold War confrontations of the 1950s and 1960s.

That vision, of a world made safe and prosperous by the collective action of all nations, explains the enduring power of what former secretary of defense and head of the World Bank Robert McNamara called "Wilson's ghost." The spread of freedom and democracy, most Americans believe, would benefit everyone, and at the same time, a free, democratic world would be one in which the United States would be secure and American goods and services would be welcomed eve-rywhere. The question of whether collective international action, such as Wilson advocated, or unilateral American policy will be most conducive to the creation of the sort of world Americans want is the basic foreign policy issue of the early twenty-first century, as it was of the early twentieth century.

Key Lessons:

Keep Reinventing Yourself

Life's not static. Neither are you. Embrace your changes and make them work for you. Life is a continuous process of reinvention. Sometimes, it means becoming more of who you are. Sometimes, it means becoming more of who you were born to be. Other times, it means choosing more of who you want to be.

Do More Of What You Love

One of the best questions a mentor once asked me was: "What do you want to spend more time doing?" I had been so wrapped up in figuring out my career moves that I lost sight of the basics. After thinking it over, I got clarity around the things I liked to do the most. This made choosing my next moves a lot easier, be-cause I now knew what I wanted to fill my day with. Figure out what you want to spend more time doing. Then, find a way to do more of it.

Model The Best

"If I have seen further it is by standing on the shoulders of giants." – Isaac Newton

You can start from scratch or you can start from examples. By starting from examples, you can "Stand on the shoulders of giants" and leapfrog ahead. More importantly, you can use the examples to model from and inspire and guide yourself with skill. They will help you avoid dead ends and glass ceilings.

You can always choose to ignore what other people have done. But that should be an explicit decision. One of the best ways to speed up success is to build on the patterns and practices that work. Success always leaves clues. You can learn from the success of others to tune and prune your own success path.

Use Mentors As The Short-Cuts

Mentors are the ultimate short-cut. Find mentors who have "been there, done that." They can shave years off your journey and help you avoid dead ends. The best mentors will know how to tailor their experience and insight in a way that helps you play to your strengths and accelerate your success.

Break The Loop

Our little loops can make us or break us. Whether it's an action or a thought, if it doesn't serve you, break the loop. Don't dig the ruts deeper. When the loop starts, catch yourself and choose whether you need to start, stop, or continue some-thing. It's easier said than done, but awareness it the first step.

Build Better Habits

As the saying goes, "First, you make habits, and then your habits make you."

Your routines and rituals can serve you well. Your daily little actions add up over time for the compound effect. Do something once or twice and it's a one off. Do it three times, and you might be on to something. Do it for 21 days in a row, and it just might stick.

Be careful in your little choices. The thoughts you think, the things you drink, the stuff you eat, and the little things you do. Habits can be insidious and act like a slippery slope.

Do The Opposite

Sometimes the best thing you can do is to "do the opposite" of what you'd normally do, to periodically surprise people and have them see you in a new way. It's easy in life to fall into routines that don't serve us. The fastest way to change our game is to rattle our own cage and shake things up. If you're always late, try being early. If you're always slow, try changing your pace. If you're always fast, then try slowing down. If you're the person that always says, "No" to things, try saying more "Yes."

If You Always Find What's Wrong With Things, Try Finding What's Right.

If you lack your confidence, try strutting more of your stuff. Doing the opposite of what you normally do, might lead to your next best breakthrough. Worst case, you'll learn more about you, you'll learn more about balance, and you'll put more options under your belt for how you show up or how you respond in life.

Find Your Arena For Your Best Results

For 45 minutes, a violinist played his heart out in a subway station. During that time, thousands of people walked by. No applause. No recognition. Two days earlier, that same violinist, Joshua Bell, one of the world's best musicians, sold out at a theater in Boston where the seats average $100.mIn the one arena, no-body appreciated his performance. Nobody expected the world's best musician to be performing right there in front of them in a subway station. Change the arena, and suddenly Bell's world-class performance is recognized and rewarded.

As my one mentor put it to me, "You can't be a preacher in your home town." Sometimes you have to change your container. You might be the world's worst boxer, but the bar's best bouncer. Maybe you're a lousy novelist, but the word's best children's author. Maybe you're a second-rate teacher, but one of the world's best entrepreneurs. The ugly duckling wasn't so ugly when he found out he was actually a Swan. Don't be a fish out of water. When you're in your element, it's night and day.

Root Yourself in Your Mission, Not Your Position

Jobs change. Missions are durable. If you lose your job, you can find other ways to live your mission. For example, if my mission was to help people live healthier lives, but if, for whatever reason, I couldn't be a doctor, I would find other ways.

Live Without Regrets

Go for it. "It is not the things we do in life that we regret on our death bed. It is the things we do not. Find your passion and follow it." — Randy Pausch

"Did I live, did I love, did I matter?" – Brendan Burchard

"Our lives are defined by opportunities, even the ones we miss." — F. Scott Fitzgerald

"You get this one moment to regret all the things you said you'd do but never did, and then it's over. You die or you live. If you live, the look in your eyes is never the same." — Gabrielle Bouliane

Take the High Road

Don't get sucked into other people's drama. Don't get sucked into your own drama. Don't spiral down into name calling, and blaming. Step away from it. Seek higher ground. Don't get pulled down, or stoop to their level.

Govern Yourself

Apply business skills to life. Business can teach us a lot. The most important thing they can teach us is how to be sustainable. You can use the same tools that create a strong, sustainable business, to create a strong, sustainable life.

If you know your vision, mission, and values, you have a strong foundation. Strategy skills teach us how to make the most of what we've got in terms of time and resources. We can innovate in our lives to do things better, faster, cheaper, much the same way we innovate in business. We can also reflect on and improve our performance in more objective ways, much the way a business does.

Treat Work As Your Ultimate Form Of Self-Expression

Work is a great place to show up how you want to be. It's your chance to make your soul sing. It can be your ultimate dojo for personal development and your arena for your best results. If you want to be an artist, do more art on the job. You're an individual with a unique set of strengths, weaknesses, and experiences. Maybe only your closest friends know your true strengths. Maybe you don't show your strengths at work. Why not? No matter what the task is, you can leave your mark.

Made in the USA
Middletown, DE
17 October 2018